Nelson, Hitler and Diana

Admiral Lord Nelson

A wax image made in his lifetime by Catherine Andras

Nelson, Hitler and Diana

Studies in Trauma and Celebrity

Richard D. Ryder

imprint-academic.com

Published in the UK by
Imprint Academic, PO Box 200, Exeter EX5 5YX, UK

Published in the USA by
Imprint Academic, Philosophy Documentation Center
PO Box 7147, Charlottesville, VA 22906-7147, USA

ISBN-13: 978184540 166 5

A CIP catalogue record for this book is available from the British Library and US Library of Congress

To

Louis Dudley Ryder

Contents

Illustrations

Acknowledgements

I am grateful to Jeffrey Simmons, G. F. Newman, Rebecca Hall, Jon Wynne-Tyson, Julian Alexander, Kay Dunbar, Alison Weir, Barbara Gardner, Anthony Freeman, Mavis Cheek, Dr Ian Mortimer, Toby Buchan and Professor A.C. Grayling.

In particular I would like to thank to two psychiatrist friends, Dr Michael Hession and Dr Robert Oxlade, for discussing all three of my subjects in considerable depth and for their professional insight. Together with Alison Taylor and Mary Hession we enjoyed a full case conference on Adolf Hitler, while sipping gin beside the calm waters of Poole Harbour. Later I spent similarly pleasant evenings with Professor Nicholas Rodger and the late Dr Colin White discussing the life of Horatio Nelson.

When it came to German translation I relied upon my old friend Hugh Denman. Henry Ryder has also helped me and Dr Emily Ryder has given encouragement, as did Heathcote Williams, while Penny Merrett, as usual, did the real work.

Sir William Beechey's (1755-1839) Portrait of Sir William Hamilton (1730-1803), on page 14, is in the Jay and Jean Kislak Collection and is reproduced courtesy of Sotheby's Picture Library.

Preface

This book is about the power of a mother's love and what happens when a mother is lost. Such loss can have extraordinary consequences not only upon the child but upon the world at large. All three of my subjects were driven to become great celebrities and all lived lives that still considerably affect our own today – being those of the archetypal hero, the utter villain and the beautiful princess. They are among the most influential icons of our age. All of them have already been studied in depth by professional historians but none, previously, has been retrospectively analysed psychologically as I have attempted to do. In this trilogy I am seeking to make psychodynamic and diagnostic sense of the facts presented. Applying my working habits as a psychologist I focus, therefore, on the early lives of my subjects and on their relationships within their families, exploring their own words and those of witnesses. It is a matter of looking for psychological clues, bringing them together and testing them against other evidence. Above all, why did they really do what they did? There are truthful answers to be found to this question but they require detective work. I regard my subjects rather as I would clients or patients seeking treatment.

Psychiatrists and psychotherapists tend to function and think in a world that is slightly apart. We rarely use, for example, the stock-in-trade explanations for human behaviour much beloved by novelists; we often do not believe in them. Not only do we speak a different language but we also accept that there may be subtler and deeper reasons beneath the level of conscious rationalisation that have to be considered. For any behaviour there may be a score of possible determinants but only a handful that will be genuinely causal in each case. These are the truths that the good psychodynamicist tries to isolate and validate. And consensus is often to be found. At hundreds of 'case conferences' over the years I have known a dozen or so professionals reach agreement on what makes a patient do what they do. Such widely agreed explanations are usually in terms of the fears, traumas and loves of childhood that produce attitudes, fantasies and defences which are then applied or misapplied to situations in later life. Yet, to a large extent, day to day behaviour can be explained in terms of rational decisions taken for obvious reasons and this is true, too, of our three subjects. But underlying such routine behaviour is the hidden swell of psychodynamics that can determine the overall pattern of a life and the symbolic decisions taken at moments of crisis.

Readers may wonder why I have selected such an apparently disparate trio of subjects. Well, they have all been described in excellent biographies in recent years, and they certainly provide interesting contrasts. Strangely, they also share several remarkable features in common: all courted publicity, all were charismatic, all believed that they had been chosen by destiny, all were touched by psychopathology and all met violent and dramatic ends that sealed their legendary status—at Trafalgar, in the Berlin bunker or in the crash in Paris. Above all, the single most powerful formative event in all their lives, that caused all three of them to become the great historic figures that they are, was almost precisely the same: when young each lost their mother. Their reactions to this loss were different but, in every case, this trauma would haunt and shape the whole of their careers.

In this book I propose original psychological explanations that shed light upon Diana's death, the frustration of Napoleon's intention to invade Britain, and the reasons for the Second World War itself. These ideas are, as far as I am aware, quite new. All three of my famous subjects were superstars because all three wanted it to be that way. All were virtuosi in the arts of celebrity, finding their own routes to fame through glory, power or beauty. Nelson was in many ways a pioneer of the modern celebrity cult, while Hitler used revolutionary new methods of propaganda and Diana dealt skilfully with the unprecedented power that the visual media attained in the late twentieth century.

By treating Adolf Hitler as a human being it is not my intention in any way to belittle his wickedness. On the contrary, I hope that my approach will act as a particular warning for the future. As a psychologist, I do not approach human behaviour censoriously, seeking to condemn nor, indeed, to praise. Vices and virtues are all, for me, interesting phenomena that need to be explained. So I do not blame Diana for her caprices, nor praise Nelson for his courage, nor laboriously condemn Hitler for his utter infamy. I simply try to understand them.

So this trilogy is not a search for new data; it is an attempt to find new psychological insights the ample information already made available by some outstanding biographies. Psychobiography is a developing field that sometimes worries historians, some of whom may wish to dismiss such efforts as mere 'psychobabble'. But how can we really understand history without understanding the motives and behaviour of key historic figures? What really made them tick? With my background in experimental, forensic, social and clinical psychology, and with my knowledge of history, I try to find some answers.

Finally, and narcissistically perhaps, I confess that my three subjects are all rather special for me: I met Diana at Buckingham Palace; I am four times great nephew of Horatio Nelson; and Adolf Hitler's Messerschmidts once machine-gunned me in my pram (they missed!).

Richard D. Ryder
Exeter, 2009

Admiral Lord Nelson

A wax image made in his lifetime by Catherine Andras

Chapter 1

Horatio Nelson

1758–1805

'The thought of former days brings all my mother into my heart ... '

Horatio Nelson, May 1804.

Horatio Nelson is one of Britain's greatest heroes. In four famous battles, and in numerous smaller engagements, Admiral Nelson triumphed over the naval forces of the man who had conquered the rest of Western Europe – Napoleon Bonaparte – thus preventing the invasion of Britain. Despite losing an eye and an arm, Nelson remained courageous to the end, dying at the hour of his greatest glory and final victory, at Trafalgar.

Horatio Nelson was a kindly man who inspired the affectionate devotion of his sailors. His own reckless bravery and love of glory enthused his men, and his practice of explaining his battle tactics in advance to his officers, and giving them powers of initiative, produced supreme results from them. Yet he had other, less attractive, qualities that make his personality complex and difficult to understand. He was vain, obsequious towards royalty and unforgiving in his attitude to disloyalty.

Early life

Horatio was born on 29 September 1758, the fourth surviving child of the Reverend Edmund Nelson, Rector of Burnham Thorpe in Norfolk and his wife Catherine (née Suckling), a great niece of Sir Robert Walpole, England's first Prime Minister. Four more siblings followed him. Horatio was thus right in the middle of a large family all of whom, so we can surmise, had to compete for their parents' attention. A middle child in such circumstances is often at a disadvantage, the eldest most often feeling valued by being given 'adult' responsibilities by the parents, and the youngest commanding the greatest cosseting. Nevertheless, Horatio found a means of securing his mother's attention. According to family folklore he became recklessly adventurous, or 'game' as they then said, raiding a neighbour's garden for fruit at night, for example, undertaking a dangerous journey through heavy snow, and climbing trees for birds' eggs. Horatio had found a way to stand out from his brothers, all of whom were rather unexciting. Horatio was, according to at least one modern biographer, Colin White, probably his mother's favourite.

Edmund and Catherine Nelson had eleven children of whom three (including a previous Horatio) had died in infancy. Three more died in early adulthood. Horatio was closest to his boorish older brother William, destined to become the first Earl Nelson in 1805, and to his lively sister Catherine who was the youngest in the family.

As a baby, Horatio was considered a physically weak child, and was baptised early in case of his demise. But he was given a Walpole godfather and the favourite Walpole first name of Horatio. His early childhood was unremarkable for a child of a Norfolk clergyman in the mid-eighteenth century. He grew up in a quiet and, as he said, 'lonesome' village three or so miles inland from the sea, surrounded by salt flats, sand hills and marshland. Later, he and his brother William would be sent to be educated in the grammar school in Norwich and, later still, to one in North Walsham.

Colin White has described the young Horatio as 'a bright, engaging little boy who constantly sought attention and approval from adults and was naturally impulsive, especially in his affections'.

Tragedy struck the family at Christmas 1767 when Horatio was nine. On a bitterly cold Boxing Day Horatio's mother died, quite suddenly, aged only forty-two. Ten days later Ann, his maternal grandmother, who had been staying in the village, also died.

My central thesis is that virtually the whole of Horatio's extraordinary career can be seen as an unconscious and irrational attempt to win back the mother he had lost. He would do so by acting in ways that he knew would have pleased her—by joining the Navy and being courageous, patriotic, dutiful, and by defeating the French.

The family

Catherine, Horatio's mother, was rather plain in appearance and little is known for certain about her personality. Possibly she was forthright and rather feisty. She would have had little time for fussing her children with so many of them, so her love and approval probably had to be earned. Nevertheless, she was clearly a good wife and mother, and quite a forceful and practical woman. She may also have been vivacious, rather as two of her children also were—her namesake, little Catherine, and Horatio himself. The daughter of a Norfolk rector, Horatio's mother had aristocratic connections, her mother Ann being the daughter of Sir Charles Turner and Mary Walpole of Houghton Hall. So Catherine could count among her relations the celebrated agricultural pioneer Viscount 'Turnip' Townshend, Baron Horatio Walpole of Wolterton and Sir Robert Walpole himself; hers was a family of famous achievers. Her father, the Reverend Dr Suckling, had died when she was only five, and at twenty-four she had married the Reverend Edmund Nelson, then a young curate, in 1749. She seems to have had most of the family's brains and energy, as well as their class connections.

HORATIO NELSON'S FAMILY

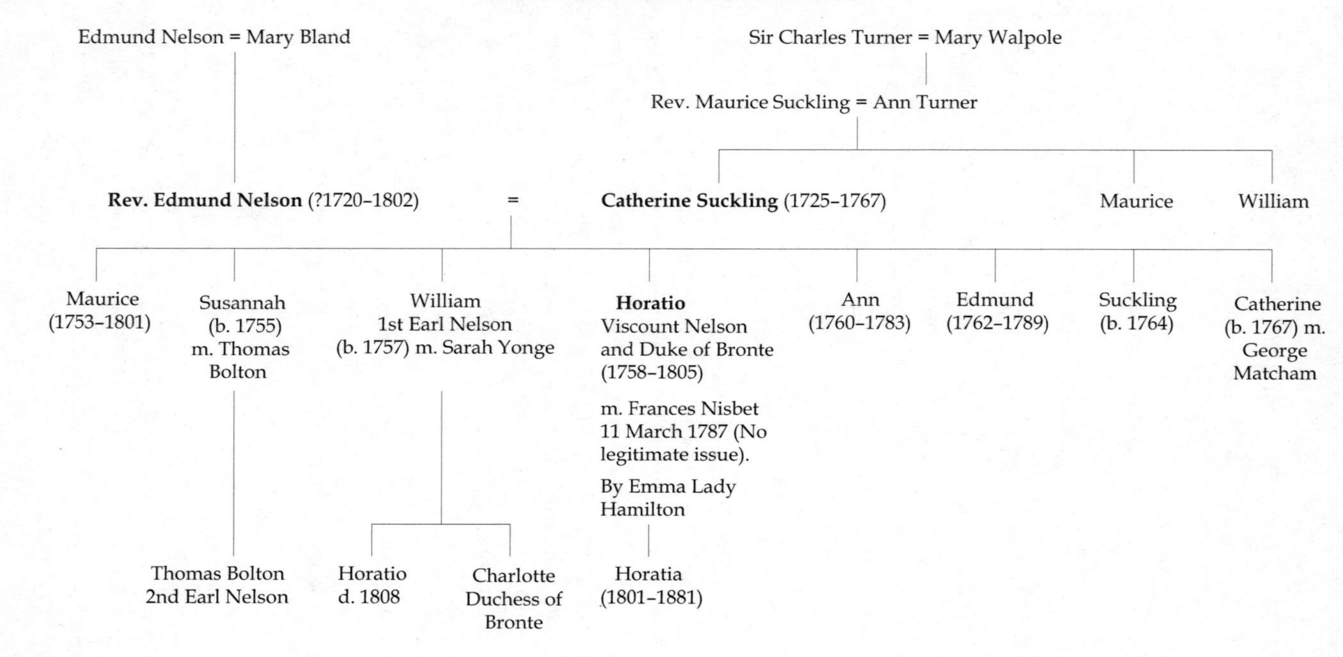

Edmund Nelson was not so well born as his wife but was a modest, kind and devout person. In later years he described himself as 'an odd whimsical old man, who knows nothing of the present time and very little of any other' and as having 'a weak and sickly constitution'. Edmund was not exactly a capable organiser nor a tower of strength; he expected his wife to do almost everything for the family and she, or her relatives, even secured him his living as a rector. After his wife's death, left with eight children to look after, he struggled incompetently to care for them, but never married again, remaining strongly loyal to his wife's memory. Horatio was not particularly close to his father, probably seeing him as rather inadequate and far duller than the members of his mother's family, such as her brothers William and Maurice Suckling. The latter, his Uncle Maurice, had become a dashing naval captain. In later years, Horatio drifted further away from his father. Although always polite to him, he did not hurry back to see him when he was ashore and, when his father died in 1802, Horatio even failed to attend his funeral, although this was partly to avoid encountering his estranged wife there. Maybe, unconsciously, Horatio held his father responsible for his mother's early demise, Edmund having burdened her with eleven births in fifteen years. There is, however, no evidence for this, although his little sister Catherine once remarked that their mother 'had bred herself to death'.

So Horatio grew up with seven siblings, three older than himself: Maurice (born in 1753), Susannah (born 1755) and William (born 1757). His four younger siblings were Ann (born 1760), Edmund (born 1762), Suckling (born 1764) and Catherine (born 1767). Another three, including a baby Horatio, died in infancy. The eldest survivor, Maurice Nelson, took after his father in personality and had a dutiful but unremarkable career in the Navy Office. The oldest daughter, Susannah, married a prosperous local businessman Thomas Bolton. William Nelson, the next child, followed his father into the church and was quite different, both physically and psychologically, from Horatio, being heavily built, loud, selfish and without charm. Among

Horatio's younger siblings, Ann became an apprentice milliner in London, had a child out of wedlock and died aged only twenty-three. Edmund and Suckling led undistinguished lives, the latter frittering away his meagre earnings on greyhounds and coursing while the former, who worked for his brother-in-law Thomas Bolton, died of tuberculosis at the age of twenty-seven. Catherine ('Kate' or 'Kitty'), Horatio's youngest sibling, was his favourite, being affectionate, vivacious and enterprising; she married the experienced traveller George Matcham in 1787.

Horatio

Horatio would, he once admitted, continue to think of his mother all his life. Although dead, she was always, psychologically speaking, with him, and his awareness of her presence was heavily laden with emotion. In a letter written in the year before he died, Horatio confessed: 'The thought of former days brings all my mother into my heart, which shows itself in my eyes.'

Horatio was aware that his mother had married beneath herself. Perhaps his lifelong quest for glory was partly an attempt to regain for his mother her true social standing by himself achieving titles and acclaim. He may have felt this was her birthright and his; social class was a matter of huge importance at the time. By giving him the Walpole name of Horatio his mother had, as it were, singled him out as one of her own. Maybe she had even indicated to him that she hoped he would honour the Walpole history of outstanding achievement. Actually doing so would be the best sort of present that a little boy, desperate to regain her love and approval, could give to the mother who had deserted him. It seems that he fantasised that such achievement could, somehow, bring her back. Furthermore, if he died in the attempt, he might, after all, see her again in heaven. Such half-conscious and entirely irrational fantasies can be very powerful.

It was Horatio's mother's younger brother, Captain Maurice Suckling, that she had admired so much. He too, in

1770, was in mourning (he had recently lost his wife—a Walpole cousin), and it was to this upper class and childless uncle that the forlorn Horatio turned in his hour of need. Clearly, if his dead mother's approval was to be won back then he should emulate the one male figure she had obviously admired and adored—her dashing naval brother with the Walpole connections. The young and bereaved Horatio initiated the approach to his uncle, asking to join the Navy. Captain Suckling was surprised that it was Horatio rather than one of his more physically robust nephews who was applying to be provided for in this way, blithely remarking, 'What has poor Horatio done, who is so weak, that he, above all the rest, should be sent to rough it out at sea? But let him come, and the first time we go into action a cannon-ball may knock off his head, and provide for him at once!' So, in April 1771 Horatio was duly admitted as a midshipman on board his uncle's ship *HMS Raisonable*. Both uncle and nephew were to do well; the former becoming Comptroller of the Navy before dying in 1778.

The young Horatio always had a sense of his own importance. He felt he was a man of destiny. Even as a junior officer he never hesitated to write letters to those in command and, when an admiral, he sought and obtained quite frequent meetings with the high and mighty, even with William Pitt the Prime Minister. Later, he lapped up the praises lavished upon him by Emma Hamilton, posed repeatedly for portraits, ensured that his brave exploits were widely reported in the press, and wallowed in the applause of the British public.

Like many highly successful and famous people, Horatio had access to surprising reserves of energy, both physical and mental. Under stress, or the excitement of the occasion, he would glitter, becoming the magnetic centre of attention. As we shall see, both Diana Spencer and Adolf Hitler had this trait too. Instead of being subdued by events all had the capacity to switch on a mental turbo-charger. This rather *hypomanic* potential is largely genetic in origin. Horatio was certainly not without fear in battle. Far from it. But he had this capacity to rise above it by experiencing 'a sudden glow' of almost ecstatic courage, believing he would die only in God's good time. His impulsive enthusiasm, informality, boyish energy and his 'wonderful mind' were often remarked upon by contemporaries, and all are parts of this temperament. Such hypomanic capacity is probably the secret ingredient in the lives of many outstanding people, providing surges of extra drive when required, as well as the star-dust of their charisma.

An outline of Horatio's career

Horatio duly joined the Navy as a midshipman, aged only twelve, and saw early service in the Arctic and the West Indies. He nearly died of malaria in 1775. At the age of twenty-one he was promoted to post-captain but was again seriously ill in 1780. Appointed in 1781 to his first command, *HMS Albemarle*, he saw action off the coast of North America. As ADC to another young officer, Prince William, he was influenced by his royal friend into marrying an older woman, the widowed Frances Nisbet, in Nevis in 1787. Frances, unexciting and unmotherly, found the weather cold when they returned to England as, for six years, they lived together in Norfolk on Horatio's half-pay.

During these unhappy years Horatio found himself out of favour with the Admiralty and King George III for having sided with Prince William in a dishonourable dispute with a fellow officer. In 1793, Horatio was at last given a further command and sailed to the Mediterranean where he first met the British Ambassador in Naples, Sir William Hamilton, and his bosomy young wife Emma. Emma, of working class origins, and an ex-mistress to several members of the aristocracy, entertained the company with her singing and dramatic performances. In 1794 Horatio led a rash attack on Corsica where he was wounded, losing the sight of his right eye. In 1797 he distinguished himself at the Battle of Cape St Vincent, was knighted and promoted to Rear-Admiral. After this battle he ensured that his exceptionally daring exploits would be widely reported in England by sending accounts of them to his old comrade

William Locker, urging that he get them published. Later in the year Horatio recklessly attacked Tenerife and lost his right arm, returning home to be nursed by his wife, and enjoying a few months of rare closeness to her. In 1798 Horatio was appointed to command a squadron in the Mediterranean, and almost totally destroyed the French fleet at the Battle of the Nile, where he received a shrapnel wound to the head. He returned to Naples to be nursed by Emma, Lady Hamilton. Horatio, now Baron Nelson of the Nile, proceeded to rescue the Neapolitan Royal Family (and the Hamiltons) from the advancing French forces, transferring them to Palermo. In June 1799 he recaptured Naples and treated highhandedly various local politicians who had collaborated with the French, permitting a number to be executed. The grateful King of Naples duly created Horatio Duke of Bronte in Sicily. Horatio had acted oddly and a little out of character at this time. Maybe he was showing signs of what today might be called post traumatic stress disorder and even, after his head wound in Egypt, the effects of frontal lobe brain damage. As Robert Oxlade has pointed out, such concussions can cause character change, irritability and moral blunting that could explain his ruthless attitude towards the Neapolitan rebels.

In 1800, again unpopular with the Admiralty, Horatio was recalled home and travelled with the Hamiltons across Europe, fêted all the way, in what was an obvious *ménage à trois*, to be warmly received by the British public on his return. He lapped up all the attention and encouraged it. Horatio and the Hamiltons were now some of the most famous people in Europe and Napoleon himself became one of Horatio's most fervent admirers, installing a bust of him on his dressing table. At Christmas 1800, Horatio separated from his wife and was promoted Vice Admiral. In April 1801 Emma gave birth to his daughter Horatia shortly before he sailed to the Baltic, where his guile and determination won the Battle of Copenhagen. From the end of that October until May 1803 Horatio was based, together with the Hamiltons, at his newly purchased home at Merton Place in Surrey. Together they toured Wales and the Mid-

Catherine Nelson
Horatio's mother, who died suddenly when he was nine.

Sir William Hamilton who became Horatio's surrogate father. This portrait by Sir William Beechey was commissioned by Nelson at Christmas 1801 and presented by him to the sitter.

Emma Hamilton
Sir William's wife and Horatio's lover.

lands. In April 1803 Sir William died in Emma's arms, Horatio holding his hand. Horatio then returned to the Mediterranean to blockade the French throughout 1804, intimidating the French Navy sufficiently to sabotage Napoleon's plans for the invasion of England. Horatio returned for his last visit to Merton in August 1805 to spend just four weeks with Emma and Horatia. He then joined *HMS Victory*, defeating the combined Spanish and French fleets at Trafalgar on 21 October 1805, and dying of a musket wound as the battle concluded. In 1806 Horatio's body was buried in St Paul's Cathedral and he was acclaimed Engand's greatest hero. Historians agree that Horatio was a charismatic leader, a recklessly brave warrior and a clever tactician.

But what was it that drove him on? Where did his extraordinary courage, patriotism and sense of duty originate? How did he inspire such loyalty and devotion in his men? Did all these traits link, somehow, with the devastating loss of his mother at Christmas 1767?

Some contradictions

Many aspects of Horatio Nelson's personality have puzzled historians and his life was full of apparent contradictions. He was kind and sensitive, yet he was brave to the point of foolhardiness and, as we have seen, ruthlessly put down acts of sedition and disloyalty in Naples. Although Horatio adored honours and royalty he never lacked the common touch, unusually for the times shaking the hands of ordinary sailors. Despite his love of titles, he was quite unsnobbish for an Englishman of his era; the informality and empathy he showed to all ranks often surprised people. Horatio was a careful planner but could also be impulsive and reckless. He longed for peace yet, untypically for the era, sought the utter destruction of his enemy's ships. In victory he insisted upon magnanimity and gentleness, and yet in battle he personally led boarding parties and took flagrant risks that were unnecessary for an officer of his seniority. He was conservative politically yet introduced novel forms of management and fairly unusual battle-tactics, creating a feeling of trust and enthusiasm among his men and fellow officers, explaining his battle plans to the latter in advance over dinner. He was conventional in social outlook and yet lived openly in an extraordinary and adulterous ménage à trois with the Hamiltons, defying the norms of the polite society to which he aspired. He loved his celebrity and yet, by the time he had settled at Merton with Emma, he was described as being quiet and unobtrusive. How can we begin to explain such paradoxes in the character of one of Britain's most famous heroes? In particular, what were the causes of Horatio's extravagant courage, extraordinary charisma and excessive sense of patriotic duty?

To understand someone fully, one has to consider nature as well as nurture. Horatio's sensitivity and empathy for others were, surely, partly genetically determined. Whereas other, more robust, sailors may have reacted to hardship by becoming hardened, the young Horatio did not. Instead, he became permanently sensitised to the sufferings of others—a factor that was to endear him to his men in future years. He detested, for example, the cruelty of a bull fight he saw in Cadiz, in June 1793. Indeed, stories abound as to his kindness. When an officer's son was arrested for rowdy behaviour by foreign authorities Horatio secretly paid the fine to have the boy released; when a sailor was distressed to have missed posting a letter home by the mail boat, Nelson ordered that the boat return specially for this one letter; a nephew said in later years that Horatio 'was anxious to give pleasure to everyone about him, distinguishing each in turn by some act of kindness and chiefly to those who seemed to require it most'.

Psychodynamics

Horatio once said that he constantly thought of his mother, yet in adulthood he could recall few details of her. This was probably a defence, as it may have been too painful for him to do so. Two points about her he did recall, however: that she had hated the French and loved the Navy. He must have concluded that these clues indicated the way to her heart. Certainly, it was the way he was to follow with sublime success. As a child he had seen his relations preparing for a French invasion of his native East Anglia in the 1760s. By fighting off the French it was as if, unconsciously, he could protect his patriotic mother from such a fate. Indeed, Horatio's own outstanding patriotism can partly be explained in this way. When his naval uncle Maurice died some years later Horatio imagined Maurice murmuring on his deathbed that he would 'leave Horatio' to his country—saying 'serve her well, and she'll never desert, but will ultimately reward you.' These are significantly strange words but ones that Horatio described as being no less than 'the inward monitor of my heart upon every difficult occasion'. Note the feminisation of country and the mention of desertion. Country and mother unconsciously became associated in Horatio's mind, rather as they would do for Adolf Hitler. Even the famous signal at Trafalgar—'England expects that every man will do his duty'—can be seen in this light. Horatio was obsessed by patriotic duty and detested disloyalty; these may have been attitudes that his mother had shown, but they were, at the same time, expressions of his continuing but unconscious loyalty and sense of duty to *her*. His last words, as he lay dying on HMS Victory were, repeatedly, 'Thank God I have done my duty'. His constant references to duty, 'bequeathing' and death were noticed by his contemporaries but their significance—as signs of his largely unconscious obsession with his dead mother—was missed.

Maybe, as bereaved children often do, Horatio even felt unconsciously responsible in some way for his mother's death. If so, then he also had to expiate this guilt. Robert Oxlade suggests that he may have felt unconsciously that he was contagiously lethal to others. This, too, sometimes happens in bereaved children. If so, then it might be that Horatio's exceptional and constant kindness was an attempt to counteract this perceived lethality. Somewhere in Horatio's mind 'country' meant 'mother', and 'duty' meant 'protection of mother'. Deep down he probably believed that if only he had protected her in 1767 she would not have died. Oxlade has pointed out that the egocentricity of bereaved children not only leads them to feel responsible for a parent's death but may make them believe that 'being good is a way to fend off further disasters'. I very much agree with this and I think this could be a further reason for Horatio's constant desire to be successful and to win praise. Horatio was always highly motivated to be 'a good boy', as his father used to say.

As we have seen, when Uncle Maurice Suckling had received Horatio's request to join the Navy in 1770, he had retorted humorously—'What has poor Horatio done, who is so weak, that he, above all the rest, should be sent to rough it out at sea?' It is clear that, although intrepid in spirit, the young Horatio was perceived as being physically weak. This, surely, was yet another incentive for the boy. Horatio would have to prove the opposite: he would compensate by being braver than anyone else. 'Gamely', he would lead the attacks upon the enemy and, as pieces of his weak body were shot away, he would gain not only the undying admiration of his men but, as he hoped unconsciously, of his dead mother too. Taking risks had always been the way that Horatio had secured his mother's attention as a child. Being wounded was also, surely, in his mind, a way to secure her motherly love and concern.

How was Horatio described by those who met him? Frequently he was seen as 'frail' or 'sickly', and sometimes as 'vain'. By middle age Horatio could acknowledge some of his own faults, such as his vanity, impatience and impulsiveness, and this self-knowledge made him a far better commander as the years went by. (In his youth he had sometimes been tactless and disciplinarian.) Yet more often it was his kindness, affectionate warmth, energy and boyish enthusiasm that impressed his contemporaries. As people typically do, they loved and felt inspired by the slightly manic charm. His strange and quirky dress sense, however, sometimes struck the more conventional viewer as rather shocking. Rather like General Bernard Montgomery over a century later, he wore old-fashioned, untidy and ill-fitting uniforms, sometimes sporting his decorations in a slightly ostentatious manner. What did all this mean? Why did he dress so eccentrically? Was it just little Horatio showing off again? Was he unconsciously appealing to women to take him in hand, tidy him up and care for him? Or was Horatio announcing that he was his mother's son—an aristocrat who did not have to concern himself with petty sartorial proprieties? I think that by acting as an aristocrat he could feel he was close to his mother again.

When Lavinia Spencer, wife of the First Lord of the Admiralty, met Horatio she referred to him as 'that dear little creature', rather as Rear Admiral Samuel Goodall described him as 'my little hero'. These are typical contemporary descriptions. The word 'little' is common to both and, although five foot six inches (his estimated height) was not so much below the average height as it is today, these quotations make it clear that, nevertheless, Horatio was seen as being small at the time. This is confirmed by the classic description given by *HMS Victory's* chaplain, Alexander Scott, after Trafalgar, when he said—'what an affectionate, fascinating little fellow he was'. So, too, does Miss Parry Herbert's description way back in 1785—'the little Captain of the Boreas, of whom so much has been said'. Horatio was also undoubtedly slender; his surviving clothing indicates this, as does the extraordinary contemporary wax-work by Catherine Andras, now at Westminster. Stature can be related to nutrition and, around 1800, the nutrition of the lower classes was not as good as it was for the middle and upper classes. So it is not impossible that Horatio was, indeed, well below average height for the better nourished officer class of his day. Of course, emotional as well as gastronomic deprivation can contribute to small stature. Whatever the reason, it cannot be seriously disputed that Horatio was often perceived by his contemporaries as being 'little', 'sickly' and 'weak'. These are the words they used to describe him and they surely reveal the effect that Horatio had upon the men and women whom he met. The important point, psychologically, is that such words often indicate that the speaker's protective and affectionate feelings towards Horatio had been activated.

The pecking order among boys, and the consequent development of self-image, depends to a large extent upon height and physical strength, but smaller boys are sometimes provoked into becoming especially ambitious or despotic and history is full of outstanding examples; Nelson's prime enemy, Napoleon Bonaparte, being a very good case in point. Surrounded by brothers, two of whom were older and bigger, Horatio, as a child, was at a natural disadvantage. We know, however, that he opted at an early age to play the role of the plucky risk-taker. As we have seen, this appears to have attracted his mother's attention in his childhood, and singled him out from the rest of his large but rather placid family. Bravery and recklessness, in Horatio's case, became substitutes for sheer physical size.

So Horatio was widely seen as an heroic little daredevil and he unwittingly used such perceptions to his advantage. If he had been physically big and reckless many would have written him off as foolhardy or buffoonish. But being physically little and reckless he inspired admiration and provoked a remarkable degree of protectiveness among his men. They were, he later said, 'a band of brothers'. Physically bigger brothers naturally feel protective towards smaller brothers, and so it was in Horatio's case. Big burly seamen were sometimes reduced to tears of affection in his presence.

Seeing their little brother rashly leading attacks upon the enemy their instinct was to follow and protect him. On several occasions Horatio's life was saved by his 'brothers' in this way. And the more he was wounded the more he provoked these feelings of affection and protectiveness. It was this extraordinary charisma that was Britain's secret weapon. By its means he inspired his men to acts of exceptional daring and determination that transformed mere naval efficiency into near invincibility. Of course, Horatio's leadership qualities did not just consist of his manic charm and his outstanding bravery as a little man leading from the front, but on a number of other factors too.

He cared for his men, ensuring they were well fed, entertained and given proper medical treatment. As Nicholas Rodger points out, after the Battle of St Vincent in 1797 Horatio was also gaining the reputation for being a winner. Increasingly, men began trusting in his judgement. Rodger has explained that all these factors, when combined with the Royal Navy's traditional emphases upon training and strict discipline, produced deadly results. In battle, Horatio's men would keep their nerve under fire, holding back their own salvoes until they would be fully effective. They would still operate efficiently, just as they had been trained, even when they were afraid. The combination of this discipline and their devotion to Horatio proved to be devastating for Britain's enemies.

As a naval tactician Horatio was fairly orthodox and eclectic. He was, however, outstandingly flexible and able to seize opportunities as they arose. Not only did he discuss his plans with his captains in advance and over good food, but he gave them far more encouragement and praise than censure. This was rather unusual for the times. Officers, used to fearing their admirals, were deeply moved by his trust in them. He would discuss various alternative courses of action and gave them the confidence to act flexibly in battle, on their own initiatives. Today it would be said that Horatio 'empowered' his men.

Royalty

Horatio can appear to us today to be rather embarrassing when it comes to royalty. He excessively revered royalty whenever he encountered it. Was this just the natural obsequiousness of an ambitious and insecure young man? Royalty took advantage of his servility on several occasions. The first was the occasion way back in 1786 when haughty Prince William, a slightly junior officer to Horatio, injudiciously fell out with his First Lieutenant in the West Indies and the inexperienced young Horatio quite wrongly took the Prince's side. As we have seen, this episode upset both King George III and the Admiralty and nearly cost Horatio his career. Furthermore, very much under Prince William's influence Horatio had unwisely married Fanny. Indeed, it is possible that he never loved Fanny and would not have married her if the Prince had not more or less insisted upon it. Years later, after the Battle of the Nile, Horatio found himself fêted and flattered by the King and Queen of Naples, and he went on to admire Queen Maria Carolina exceedingly, even declaring that it was his 'sacred duty' to serve this foreign monarch—despite the fact that she was, fairly obviously, a vindictive and manipulative person. Nevertheless, it was at her insistence, egged on by her friend Emma, that Horatio rashly involved the British fleet in suppressing the rebellion in Naples, broke a treaty that one of his officers had made with the rebels, and allowed 160 of them, including his old comrade-in-arms Francesco Caracciolo, to be hanged. This murky episode caused questions to be asked in the British parliament, again upset the Admiralty, and is the reason why Horatio to this day is regarded in Italy as a war criminal. When he was dealing with royalty Horatio made such mistakes. But why? He was, after all, quite prepared to ignore the orders of his superior officers—nearly always with resounding success, as when, for example, he had ignored his superior Admiral's command to withdraw at Copenhagen and went on to win the battle. He disobeyed them because he put his country (mother) first. But when it came to royalty, he became slavishly obedient. Of course, at the time, royalty was royalty. The divine right of sovereigns was still widely accepted and European royalties still exercised real power. However, Sigmund Freud would later suggest that, when some of his nineteenth-century patients dreamed of kings or queens, these figures were often disguised representations of their fathers and mothers. Is it too fanciful to suggest that Horatio, too, maternally obsessed as I believe he was, unconsciously saw Queen Maria Carolina as a representation of his mother? If so, it is hardly surprising that he went to such lengths to protect her, rescue her from the French and to take revenge upon those who were disloyal to her. Very probably he also saw Emma as, in some regards, an extension of the Queen, and was showing off to her. Not only had Emma become a confidante of Queen Maria Carolina but the Queen had actually ordered Emma to act on her behalf and in her interests when dealing with the British admiral. This could be another reason why Horatio fell for Emma who quickly became, in so many ways, his rediscovered mother.

Horatio's extreme sense of patriotic duty

Horatio's excessive reverence for royalty was tied up with his extreme patriotism, his outstanding sense of duty and with his detestation of treason and disloyalty. Rather as with Hitler, Horatio's kindness quickly disappeared with those whom he saw as traitors. Loyalty was everything for Horatio, albeit loyalty to country rather than to himself personally. What was the origin of this behaviour? This is one of the hardest aspects of Horatio's personality to decipher.

If Horatio was a patient of mine today I would want to explore his possible feelings of guilt and anger over his mother's death. Was getting himself wounded not only an unconscious attempt to win his mother's love but also a means to punish himself for what he felt was his responsibility for her demise? These sorts of feelings may appear very strange and irrational to some readers but they are surprisingly common among bereaved children, and could have been present in Horatio's case, as both Oxlade and Hession have confirmed.

As a psychologist, one becomes used to discovering the exact opposite to what is first presented. Horatio presents us with his great sense of duty, with his hatred of disloyalty and with his extreme patriotism. He throws all this in our face, constantly. I have already speculated that England and his mother became connected in his mind and that patriotism, therefore, unconsciously represented his love for his mother. But why did he so often emphasise all this? Could it all be a defence—a concealment even from himself—of exactly the opposite sorts of feelings: of rebellious anger against his mother? Was his exaggerated sense of duty towards her a way of concealing his unconscious fury with her for deserting him by dying? It seems that Horatio protests his duty far too much! Sometimes we are particularly upset by those who remind us of our own secret or barely conscious feelings or failings. Is this why Horatio, who was otherwise so kind, could be so punitive towards those whom he saw as disloyal to his foreign queen in Italy?

Conclusions

It seems to me that Horatio never really grew up. He was always the little boy bereaved. He was always stuck at Christmas 1767, looking for someone to care for him. In his wife, except for a few months when, significantly, she had nursed him after he lost his arm in 1797, he had failed to find the mother he yearned for. It was to Emma Hamilton and her billowy embrace that he finally and rapturously came home emotionally, falling in love, equally significantly, as she nursed him after he had been wounded at the Battle of the Nile in the following year. Nursing, as an emblem of maternal affection, was what Horatio had always needed, and he needed it especially at that time when he was showing marked signs of what today might be called post traumatic stress disorder after the shattering battle of the Nile. Emma gave him motherly love in bucketfuls and intuitively responded to his hunger for approval by heaping praises upon him, often to an absurd degree, and putting up portraits of him everywhere she could, both in Naples and later at Merton. Besides, Horatio had, literally, rescued Emma from the French advance in 1798, just as he had probably fantasised he would rescue his real mother. He had thus earned and won her love. He felt redeemed. The contented ménage à trois with Sir William Hamilton merely served to reinforce this parental ambience, and to such an extent that Sir William psychologically replaced his real father at this time. Sir William not only provided the aristocratic feeling that was associated with his mother, but also treated Horatio affectionately as the son he had never had. (Sir William was twenty-eight years older than Horatio, who was only seven years older than Emma.)

Horatio very obviously transferred his family relationships on to his close associates in later life. As orphaned and half-orphaned children often do, the Nelson siblings had become mutually supportive, Horatio pairing up with his older brother William. They could not fully rely upon their well-meaning but weak and incompetent father. They had gone off to school together in Norwich, William taking the role of 'the heavy' while spindly little Horatio seems to have played 'the brains'. In effect, Horatio became the leader of the pair; he was the risk-taker and the entrepreneur. This role-play continued throughout Horatio's naval career as he transformed a number of his captains into 'bigger brothers'; the hefty Captain Thomas Hardy of *HMS Victory* being the most obvious example. As Colin White has pointed out, Horatio also found several 'father figures' during his adult life, among them Lord Hood, Sir Peter Parker, Lord St Vincent and, finally, Sir William Hamilton. Most were physically bigger and considerably older than Horatio and he provoked in them a kind of paternal protectiveness. Unlike his real father these were all strong and highly capable men. Horatio, was, in many ways, a lifelong child who tended to turn others into surrogate siblings and parents. This was the other quintessential ingredient of his charisma. We all tend to replay our childhoods in later life, projecting our childhood families onto the big screen of the wider world, but Horatio did it to perfection and on a grand scale. So the whole Navy became his family, where he found the paternal and fraternal supports he needed. He even had some 'sons' such as William Hoste and poor John Weatherhead who was killed in action. As I have stressed, his chief motive in life, although unconscious, was to win back the love of his mother who had died when he was young. This was actually impossible, of course, but the unconscious mind often works irrationally in this way, expressing core fears and fundamental wishes, regardless of reality. It seems that Horatio unconsciously identified his mother with his country, and so, by fighting off the French (whom she had said she hated), he and his band of brothers could protect and rescue his mother (England). Whenever Horatio refers to his country one can substitute the word 'mother'. It proves a fascinating exercise, and often makes better sense of what may otherwise appear to be Horatio's excessive patriotism.

Horatio was a prolific letter writer, the words flowing almost uncensored from the heart, spelling mistakes and all, and often revealing very frankly his feelings and ambitions. Through these letters he kept in touch with his old friends over the years. His love letters to Emma reveal his sexual as well as his affectionate feelings for her. It is through many of these five thousand surviving letters that his character emerges—direct, enthusiastic, ambitious, conservative, patriotic, kindly, flamboyant, attention-seeking, dynamic, daring, sentimental, affectionate and, of course, obsessed by duty. Themes of death, legacy, ill-health, and destiny are frequent. 'Humanity after victory', too, is often a theme—such as in his 1804 instruction—'It is the duty of individuals to soften the horrors of war as much as possible.' Throughout his life he kept writing to his brothers and sisters; his sense of family never left him.

The whole of his career can be seen as a desperate attempt by Horatio to replay the family experiences of his childhood so that, instead of with the tragedy of his mother's death, it would all end happily the second time around. And for Horatio it did—when he had repeatedly defeated the French, he fell in love with the seductive yet motherly Emma Hamilton and died before that relationship itself could turn sour. Emma resembled his mother in several ways: she was, for example, physically strong; indeed, both women have been described as being 'statuesque'. She was certainly physically larger than Horatio. More importantly, both were good practical organisers and Emma had hugely impressed him by sensibly and calmly organising the panicky Sicilian royals during their escape by sea to Palermo in December 1798, in one of the fiercest storms Horatio had ever known. Emma was what psychologists sometimes call 'the good mother': she flattered, nursed and idolised Horatio. Her love was unconditional. Fanny, Horatio's wife, on the other hand, had failed to realise that he needed this mothering. She did not see his baby side and was, herself, looking for parental love (which she found, to an extent, in Nelson's father). Even worse, Fanny could not understand Horatio's need for fame and flattery. So she had inadvertently starved him of these emotional essentials. He had also felt an outsider as regards the 'establishment' of his day; an establishment that he was always trying to join. The Hamiltons made him feel part of this establishment. Emma was, above all, a booster of his fragile self-esteem, a 'rewarder of his exploits', as White puts it, just as his mother might have been. Like many love-starved children Horatio had fantasised an 'ideal family' and the ménage à trois appeared to re-create this perfection that Horatio had never actually known. This is why Horatio ignored the disapproval of polite society and brazenly flaunted the ménage: he saw it not as a scandalous sexual arrangement but as his happy family, at last discovered.

Is it fair to burden Horatio with a modern psychiatric label? Was his personality sufficiently abnormal or his performances in love or in his career significantly impaired? No, they were not. Nevertheless, he was highly unusual—and Britain may have owed her political survival to this fact. Remarkably—and perhaps controversially, Horatio shared some features in common with Adolf Hitler in that, even from his adolescence, he believed he was special, that he should associate with high-status people, and in being preoccupied with ideas of outstanding personal achievement. Horatio also believed he was a man of destiny. Furthermore, he was extremely vain and enjoyed excessive admiration. These are all characteristics of a *narcissistic personality*. But this is not quite the same as saying he had a significant *disorder*. To have a personality *disorder* means that one's personality causes suffering to oneself or trouble to associates, either socially or in one's occupational life, or both. Furthermore, people with real personality *disorders* have difficulty in responding adaptively and flexibly to changing circumstances. None of this is true of Horatio. On the contrary, his personality did not cause him constant suffering, his social life, although unorthodox, was often satisfying, and his career was spectacularly successful. What is more, he showed considerable flexibility and learned from his mistakes. Despite repeated battle traumas of great intensity, the physically frail Horatio displayed extraordinary mental toughness and agility. Following the loss of his beloved mother when he was nine one might have anticipated a typical depressive reaction. Maybe there was one but it is not recorded. Instead, we see Horatio's determination to join the Navy and fight the French, and I have suggested that this is a fantasied quest for the return of his lost mother. This is Horatio's highly unusual solution to the insoluble agony of his bereavement. Like Adolf Hitler, and, indeed, Princess Diana, his reaction to the loss of an adored mother became central to the remainder of his life. It was a fascinating and remarkable reaction and, as it so happened, of huge historic importance for Britain and the world.

Some final thoughts

What would have happened if Horatio had not taken that final step on Victory's quarter deck? The musket ball would have missed him and he might have survived Trafalgar. But what then? Well, he would still have been England's hero. Even the hostile King George would have had to make him a duke and would have given him a decent pension. Initially Horatio would have insisted upon retirement from active service. But for how long would he have remained contented? With Emma by his side he would have endlessly milked the applause at public events. Since meeting the Hamiltons he had developed a taste for the theatre and I am sure they would have gone frequently to the latest shows at Drury Lane and Covent Garden. But sooner or later the old boredom would have set in and he would be asking some future Prime Minister for work. In his last few years Nelson had developed quite remarkable skills as an administrator and I can see him being tempted by the post of First Lord of the Admiralty when old Lord Barham finally retired in 1806. Perhaps, this would have been too soon for him, particularly if he had decided to visit and repair his estates at Bronte in Sicily: he would have found he had more than enough to do there, under the slopes of Etna.

Would the relationship with Emma have lasted? Yes, I think it would. Emma was losing her looks and would never have been seriously tempted to find another man. She, too, loved being a celebrity. Being with Horatio would also give her very considerable protection against the sneers and snobbery of society. She craved respectability. The Prince of Wales had once or twice quite openly flirted with Emma but this amorous threat never materialised after Horatio's death and so is unlikely to have done so if he had lived. Besides, Horatio and Emma loved each other and their child, Horatia. Horatio, feeling safe with Emma, would go through a period of deep child-like dependency on her. Her extravagance would be a problem, but an affluent double duke might not have found this too difficult to manage. Living with the melodramatic and gin-swilling Emma might prove to be a strain at times but he could always get away to his office at the Admiralty or, in extremis, take a trip to Bronte, if she became impossible. All in all, I think the Duke of Merton and Bronte would have settled down and, provided he did not try his hand at politics as other war veterans such as Wellington would do, would have remained a contented hero, surrounded by admirers and his extended family.

As with Adolf and Diana, Christmas time was often a problem for Horatio. His mother had died at Christmas in 1767. After that he tended, so it seems to me, to be ill or to behave oddly or significantly at Christmasses generally. John Sugden notes that Horatio's old father was also affected at this season; at Christmas 1797, for instance—thirty years after his wife Catherine's death—he was still mourning her and blaming himself, all too accurately, for being an inadequate parent. It was at Christmas 1798 that Horatio rescued the Hamiltons and the Sicilian royals and took them to Palermo, beginning to fall in love with Emma at that time. Their sexual liaison probably started at Christmas 1799, a year later. It was also at Christmas—in

1800—that Horatio abruptly separated from his wife Fanny and went to Torquay, via Fonthill, where he had 'such a spasm of the heart' that he thought he would die. Sugden also inadvertently reveals that there was a further childhood precedent for this timing—at Christmas 1770 his father had left his unhappy children in the cold Norfolk rectory while he selfishly went off to Bath for a holiday. This was only three years after they had lost their mother, and this feeling of lack of strong support from his father is almost certainly one reason why Horatio was covertly angry with him. Oxlade, together with Michael Hession, while supporting my general thesis, also points out that the age of a lost parent at the time of their death can become a conscious or unconscious source of dread for a bereaved child, who may act significantly when other loved ones, or they themselves, approach more or less the same age, as if fearing a repetition of their tragic loss. In Nelson's case, his mother had died when she was forty-two. Nelson himself reached this age in 1800—just as he decided to separate from his wife and transfer all his love to Emma. At the same time his wife Fanny was approaching forty while Emma claimed to be several years younger so may, unconsciously, have appeared to Nelson to provide better prospects of survival—'the little Horatio might well believe that the age of forty-two was significant and could well prove disastrous', as Hession puts it. In the event, Nelson would die in 1805 when Emma was probably forty-two, although she claimed to be forty.

I think we lack sufficient evidence as to why Horatio found his own father ultimately psychologically inadequate, although experiences such as the Christmas abandonment of 1770 were, surely, part of the reason. Maybe, as psychoanalysts would say, his Oedipal attachment to his mother had made Horatio antagonistic towards his father. The old man was certainly rather dull and middle-class while Horatio clearly craved excitement and aristocracy. His father also had a tendency to 'flap' at moments of minor crisis (a trait probably despised by his battle-scarred son), and was sometimes melancholic and hypochondriacal. So

Horatio unconsciously may have felt he had to replace his ineffectual father by himself becoming the family's reliable breadwinner and protector: hence his incessant attempts to forward the interests and careers of his parasitic brothers. Nevertheless, Horatio still wished to find a strong and effective father for himself. So it was in Sir William Hamilton that he eventually found an altogether more psychologically satisfactory parent: worldly-wise and, above all, aristocratic. Sir William seems to have impressed Horatio just as much as did Emma when first they met. Indeed, I will go further and suggest that it was Sir William who actually changed Horatio and gave him a wholly new outlook on life. Horatio, like most naval officers at the time, had hardly had a secondary education—except in gunnery, discipline and nautical knots. Sir William was cultured, extremely knowledgeable about art and a pioneer vulcanologist. He was also aristocratically liberal about sex. When they went on tours together Sir William would show Horatio the grand houses, the paintings and the countryside, and take him to the theatres. All these were new experiences for Horatio. His improved performance as an admiral and administrator after 1800, to which Colin White has drawn our attention, can, I believe, be put down partly to Sir William's influence. He provided Horatio with a far wider and more progressive perspective culturally, historically, politically and morally. Furthermore, he gave Horatio some confidence in his own intellectual powers. The ménage was, indeed, Horatio's ideal family.

As we have seen, Horatio was closest to his wife when she had nursed him after he had lost his arm. He also fell in love with Emma after she nursed him with the head wound he sustained at the Nile. Sugden mentions an incident from childhood when the eleven year old Horatio got measles at school and was nursed by a school nurse, the eighteen year old Elizabeth Gaze. There is no record of what the little boy felt towards her but Elizabeth, perhaps significantly, remembered the encounter well enough to recall it many years later. Maybe she recalled it because of the emotions that were exchanged with this particular little patient at that time. Nursing was, for Horatio, always an emblem of his yearned-for maternal love; a yearning that had driven him throughout his life.

As far as fame is concerned, we can see Horatio, in some ways, as being the first modern celebrity. There had never before been such spontaneous crowds of admirers. They followed his coach, cheered his arrival at important functions and sang songs of adulation in the streets. A monarch could attract crowds but not such ecstatic ones. Horatio was applauded in the theatres and other public places he visited. Ballads and eulogies were printed, and prints of his portraits were sold by the hundred. How had all this happened? True, there had been no such British military hero for almost a hundred years since Marlborough. But Nelson was different. He had the common touch. He also had Emma and, despite the disapproval of the king, their love-affair was widely celebrated. Above all, the press had repeatedly reported his victories, at least since the battle of St Vincent, and for the simple reason that Horatio had written glowing (but not wildly inaccurate) reports of his exploits to his friends back in England, urging them to release these accounts to the newspapers. Horatio longed for glory and promoted his own illustrious image. This was not considered to be an entirely reputable thing to do at the time, modesty being the order of the day. Again, Horatio can be seen as breaking the polite conventions of the age. He could claim, however, and with partial truth, that he did so in order to make sure that he received his fair share of prize-money, although just as important, or even more so in Horatio's case was his craving for renown. He was not using fame to project a message as Adolf Hitler would later do. Horatio, like Diana, craved celebrity almost as an end in itself. The world would then give him what his mother could no longer give—acclaim and affection.

In the last few idyllic weeks before Trafalgar, now living with Emma and their daughter, Horatio seemed to have changed. His whole career had been a quest for maternal love and approval. That quest was now achieved and he longed for retirement and childlike dependence on Emma. Lord

Minto, visiting at this time, concluded, 'he is in many points a really great man, in others a baby'. Friends thought he had put on weight and a nephew described his kindly uncle as now being 'quiet, sedate and unobtrusive'. What a change indeed! Game little Horatio had got his mother back at last.

Sources

Beatty, William, *The Authentic Narrative of the Death of Lord Nelson* (1807)

Clarke, James Stanier and M'Arthur, John, *The Life and Services of Horatio Viscount Nelson,* 2 vols (1809)

Coleman, Terry, *Nelson:The Man and the Legend* (Bloomsbury, 2001)

Fraser, Flora, *Beloved Emma* (London: Weidenfeld & Nicholson, 1986)

Harrison, James, *The Life of Horatio Viscount Nelson* (1806)

Hession, Michael, Personal Communication, April 2005.

Jarrold, R.R., *Nelson* (2003).

Nicholas, Sir Harris, *The Dispatches and Letters of Lord Nelson,* 7 vols (1844–6)

Oman, Carola, *Nelson* (Hodder & Stoughton, 1947)

Oxlade, Robert, Personal Communication, April 2005.

Oxlade, Robert, Significant Dates Replay Nelson's Traumatic Childhood Bereavement, *Trafalgar Chronicle,* 14. 2004.

Pocock, Tom, *Horatio Nelson* (Oxford: Bodley Head, 1987)

Rodger, N. A. M., Personal Communication, December 2007.

Ryder, Richard D., The Character of Horatio Nelson: A Note, *Trafalgar Chronicle,* 14. 2004.

Ryder, Richard D., Nelson's Character: A Further Note, *Trafalgar Chronicle,* 15. 2005.

Southey, Robert, *The Life of Nelson* (1813). See *Southey on Nelson,* ed. Richard Holmes (Harper, 2004).

Sugden, John, *Nelson: A Dream of Glory* (Cape, 2004).

Vincent, Edgar, *Nelson: Love and Fame* (Yale University Press, 2003)

White, Colin, ed., *Nelson: The New Letters* (Boydell Press, 2005)

White, Colin *The Nelson Encyclopedia* (Chatham, 2002)

Adolf Hitler

Chapter 2

Adolf Hitler

1889–1945

'One day the world will understand what this struggle was about.'

(Adolf Hitler, 1945)

Adolf Hitler became the leader of Germany in 1933 and cold-bloodedly caused the deaths of some six million Jews, homosexuals and gypsies in his extermination camps. He conquered or dominated almost all of Western Europe (except Britain) during the early years of the Second World War. Eventually, after invading Russia, and the loss of over forty million lives, the armies of his cruel Nazi empire were defeated by the Allies in 1945, and Adolf committed suicide. He left a scar upon the face of the world and its effects are with us still. He is widely regarded as one of the wickedest men who ever lived.

Adolf Hitler was rather a pleasant man to work for. After the war his female secretaries said he was, on the whole, a quiet and considerate employer who usually had a smile or words of encouragement for them. He urged several of them, in the final weeks, to escape from the Berlin bunker and find somewhere safer to go. Of course there were occasional tantrums—but then things were not exactly going well for the Reich. You can often judge a man by the qualities of his women, some people said, and Eva Braun was reported to be sweet-natured, brave, warm, loyal and, according to Albert Speer, intelligent. Even though he had to face repeated disloyalties among his officers, Adolf's personal vengeance was ill-defined. Often he simply demoted or transferred those who had failed him badly, and left the punishment of outright traitors to others. He despised most of his generals but usually pensioned them off, with high honours, when they let him down, or gave them extended sick leave. He might have a rant or two, but these displays were rarely followed up by specific orders for execution or cruelty. Often he would procrastinate or give directions that were ambiguous. Indeed, the Führer was sometimes so exasperatingly vague in his orders that, on occasions, his underlings more or less had to make them up. He did not really want to know about details or failures or about anything really nasty. He signed routine death warrants for cowardice but rarely initiated sentences. Stalin despised him for such 'weaknesses'. During the years he was Führer he never killed anyone himself, personally, except himself. Adolf did not look like a villain. His clothes were neat but not flamboyant. His manners towards guests were usually excellent and he often appeared to be a little shy.

For years before the war Adolf had lived in his comfortable country house at Berchtesgaden, getting up late and refusing to talk politics until even later in the day. He had certainly done well for himself. He would spend hours alone or with Eva or the dogs, playing with his architectural models of the future Berlin, discussing his health with his quack doctor, going on walks through the woods, eating chocolates and pastries, reading pornography, watching light-hearted Hollywood films and Micky Mouse cartoons, or gazing happily at the breathtaking views of the surrounding mountains. Often he ate lunch on his own. Eventually, sometimes after keeping important political visitors waiting for hours, he would make the effort to put on more formal clothes, or uniform, and emerge to dazzle them with his brilliant conversation and piercing eyes, talking late into the night about the great and glorious achievements of the future. Usually his visitors would leave far later than they had intended, but feeling inspired.

Adolf had almost always lived like this. He disliked work in the ordinary sense. He was an artist, an actor and a fantasist. He preferred ideas to reality.

The family

Adolf had been born in Braunau Am Inn in Austria on 20 April 1889. His mother Klara (from whom Adolf inherited his extraordinary blue eyes) was aged twenty-nine when Adolf was born and he was her fourth child, her three eldest having died in infancy. Already being cared for by Klara were her husband Alois' two children by a previous marriage—Alois (Junior) born 1882 and Angela, born 1883. They addressed Klara as 'mother'. So, until the age of five, the infant Adolf found himself the youngest in a family of three and, because he was his mother's only surviving child, after three infant deaths, he was, naturally, very much her favourite. At the age of five, in 1894, Adolf's privileged position was challenged when a brother Edmund was born, to be followed when Adolf was seven by a sister, Paula, in 1896. In the same year Adolf's older half-brother Alois (Junior) left home, apparently for good. So Adolf was, from the age of seven, the oldest boy in the home, with 'jolly' older half-sister (Angela), younger brother (Edmund) and 'quiet' baby sister (Paula). This situation continued until Edmund's death through illness in 1900 when Adolf was eleven. Adolf then became the only boy in the house. (Adolf would support his sister Paula financially until his death in 1945.)

Both of Adolf's parents had come from peasant stock. They were cousins, and for this reason they had had to seek authority to marry. His mother addressed his father as 'Uncle' and had been his maid before they married.

Adolf's father

Adolf's father Alois had climbed the social ladder successfully as a Customs Officer and established the family as house-owning middle class. He was clearly an ambitious

ADOLF HITLER'S CHILDHOOD FAMILY

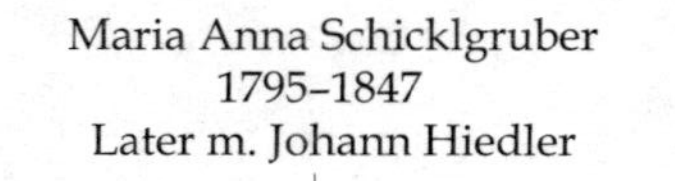
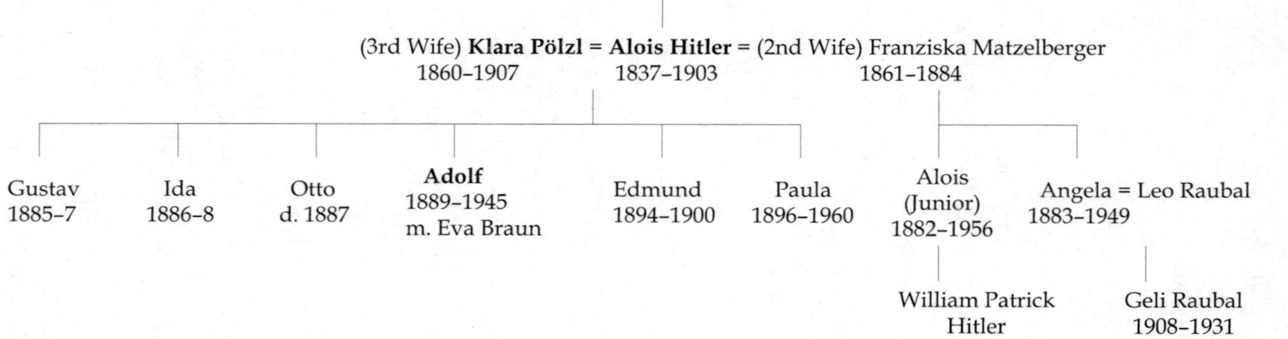

and hard-working man. Work colleagues described Alois as 'very strict, exact, even pedantic at work and a very unapproachable person'. He was also said to be humourless, pompous, and unpredictably bad-tempered. At home Alois was a stern, distant and punitive father who frequently beat his children, especially Adolf. When Paula Hitler, Adolf's little sister, was interviewed on 5 June 1946 at Berchtesgaden she recalled a family of 'very lively children who were perhaps somewhat difficult to train. If there were ever quarrels or differences of opinion between my parents it was always on account of the children. It was especially my brother Adolf who challenged my father to extreme harshness and got his sound thrashing every day.' Angela, his half-sister, also spoke of these regular beatings, and Adolf himself described his father to Joseph Goebbels in 1932 as a *haustyrann* or 'domestic tyrant'. William Patrick Hitler (Adolf's half brother's son) claimed that on several occasions both his father and Adolf were beaten unconscious by Alois, Adolf once being left for dead.Alois drank regularly and smoked heavily and was, it seems, more interested in bee-keeping than in his family. There are reports that Alois also beat his wife and his dog.

On 3 January 1903, when the abused Adolf was thirteen years old, his father collapsed and died while drinking in the local Gasthaus. Adolf, throughout his 'very painful' teens, as he later described them, was now the only man about the house. In his autobiographical *Mein Kampf* ('My Struggle') of 1924 he was to depict his father as 'a dutiful civil servant' who wanted his son to follow the same career: 'It was inconceivable to him that I might reject what had become the content of his whole life … a whole lifetime spent in the bitter struggle for existence had given him a domineering nature.' (We should note the appearance of the word 'struggle'; it often appears in Adolf's book of the same title. Later, Adolf would reveal that he believed that most civil servants were Jewish.)

So Adolf admits that he resisted his father's ambition for him:

> Then barely eleven years old, I was forced into opposition for the first time in my life. Hard and determined as my father might be in putting through plans and purposes once conceived, his son was just as persistent and recalcitrant in rejecting an idea which appealed to him not at all, or in any case very little.
>
> I did not want to become a civil servant.

Adolf is clearly proud of this resistance to his father's demands. Often dismissed by historians as an unreliable and self-promoting tract *Mein Kampf* is, nevertheless, every word of it, of interest to the psychologist. It contains much accurate and honest analysis—far more than most have imagined—mixed in with some revealing elements of falsehood, fantasy and exaggeration. Any such distortions, however, are as interesting as are the 'accuracies'. Sometimes they tell us how Adolf sees himself and how he wants others to see him. It actually comes across that, notwithstanding the conflict between them, Adolf is proud of his father's iron determination and career success. He seems even to exaggerate these qualities a little. He is also frank about his opposition to his father's wishes. As often happens in such cases of father-son conflict Adolf shows ambivalence; he rejects utterly some of his father's traits and habits, for example, his love of alcohol, tobacco, bees, exactitude, punctuality and hard work, but he incorporates and copies others—his stubbornness, determination, ambition, patriotism and, ultimately, his use of violence. Like his father, Adolf, too, would one day have a sexual relationship with a female relative.

Adolf tells us that when he eventually blurted out his ambition to become an artist, his father 'was struck speechless':

> 'Painter? Artist?'
>
> He doubted my sanity, or perhaps he thought he had heard wrong or misunderstood me… he opposed it with all the determination of his nature … 'Artist, no, never as long as I live!' But since his son, among various other qualities, had apparently inherited his father's stubbornness, the same answer came back at him. Except, of course, that it was in

> the opposite sense ... I went one step further and declared that if that was the case I would stop studying altogether.

All this rings very true. Adolf is also surprisingly honest in admitting his failure at school at this time:

> For the moment only one thing was certain: my obvious lack of success at school. What gave me pleasure I learned, especially everything which, in my opinion, I should later need as a painter. What seemed to me unimportant in this respect or was otherwise unattractive to me, I sabotaged completely.

So Adolf indicates that his academic failures were deliberate and all part of his long battle with his father. This may well have been the case. He claimed he found the schoolwork 'ridiculously easy' but preferred to play truant. He wanted his 'liberty'. Perhaps there is a hint of resentment that his father had sent him to the vocational *Realschule* rather than to the more academic *Gymnasium*, but this is not explicitly stated. At school, so Adolf says, he became argumentative:

> It was at this time that the first ideals took shape in my breast ... I believe that even then my oratorical talent was being developed in the form of more or less violent arguments with my schoolmates. I had become a little ring-leader; at school I learned easily and at that time very well, but was otherwise rather hard to handle ... But since my father, for understandable reasons, proved unable to appreciate the oratorical talents of his pugnacious boy, or to draw from them any favourable conclusions regarding the future of his offspring, he could, it goes without saying, achieve no understanding for such youthful ideas.

Adolf recalls his father's death in fairly orthodox terms, denying the feelings of relief, guilt or even of joy he might have then experienced. But he remarks with insight: 'Unwittingly he (Alois) had sown the seed for a future which at that time neither he nor I would have comprehended.

Alois' death occurred far too soon for him to resolve his conflict with his son, or for Adolf to come to terms with his father. This would prove crucial. It is hardly surprising that Adolf cannot say 'I hated my father'. He was probably not even fully aware of these feelings in himself at the time.

Alois Hitler
Adolf's bullying father.

Klara Hitler
Adolf's beloved mother, who died when he was eighteen.

Adolf Hitler as a boy

He was living in the highly mannered and inhibited culture of a small Austrian country town in the early 1890s. Only a few miles away, in Vienna, Sigmund Freud was, at that same time, reacting to similar cultural conditions by starting the psychoanalytic revolution that helped to establish a more honest depiction of human relationships, postulating that we are often unconscious of some of the most potent formative forces within us. Freud would have much to say about unconsciously-hated fathers as the source of neurosis and as part of his famous Oedipus Complex. (In Greek myth Oedipus married his mother and killed his father. See Glossary.)

Historians have speculated as to Alois Hitler's exact parentage. The consensus is that he was certainly illegitimate although Alois' father's identity remains uncertain. Alois' mother, Maria Anna Schicklgruber, had been a forty-two year old unmarried servant when Alois was born. Later she married into the Hiedler (or Hitler) family and Alois took this name. (Adolf told his friend August Kubizek years later that he was pleased about this name-change as he found Schicklgruber 'so uncouth, so boorish'.) There was the obvious possibility that Alois' father might have been partly Jewish as Maria Anna had worked for several families that either were Jewish, or at least sounded as though they were Jewish. Some said she had been employed by Baron Rothschild in Vienna and, later as a cook, by a family called Frankenberger in Graz. Furthermore, the Frankenberger family had reputedly paid regular support to Maria Anna for the upkeep of Alois until he was fourteen. According to the historian Ian Kershaw all this is without reliable foundation; there were no Jews in Graz at the time and the name Frankenberger is not necessarily Jewish. Yet Adolf certainly heard these stories, and rumours of his alleged Jewish descent circulated openly in the 1920s and 1930s. Indeed, according to the Nazi lawyer Hans Frank, Adolf asked him to investigate them in 1930. Of course, even if the Frankenbergers were, despite their name, not Jewish, Adolf could still have *believed* that they were.

August Kubizek

As far as Adolf's childhood is concerned there is one other remarkable witness—his only boyhood friend, August Kubizek—whose own memoirs confirm much of what Adolf describes. These are the main source of first hand evidence we have about the teenage Adolf. Biographies are occasionally spoiled by their authors feeling obliged to denigrate Hitler and to portray him as insincere or psychopathic. Kubizek's account does not suffer from these faults. His memoirs were initially composed during the war and then expanded, perhaps with the help of a ghost writer, in the late 1940s, being first published in 1953. Ian Kershaw concludes that although Kubizek's account is sometimes faulty as regards events—'it rings true in the portrait of Hitler's personality and mentality'. Kubizek first met Adolf in 1904, the year after Alois' death, when Adolf was fifteen, and became his close companion for the next four years, then losing touch until 1938. Kubizek describes a solitary, self-obsessed, lazy and angry boy, inhibited, shy, yet brilliantly articulate, dogmatic and bursting with ideas; in many ways Adolf appeared to be the classic 'spoiled brat'. By the time Kubizek first met him he was already essentially the Adolf Hitler of adulthood. What would change over the years would be the increased toughness he learnt in the First World war, the politicisation of Adolf in the beer-cellars of Munich and the crystallisation of his anti-semitism during the 1920s. Young Adolf needed someone to talk at. Later it would be the entire German Reich but, in 1904, Kubizek filled this role. Kubizek at once noticed that Adolf was still determined not to become a civil servant:

> There was no end to the things, even trivial ones, that could upset him (Adolf). But he lost his temper most of all when it was suggested that he should become a civil servant. Whenever he heard the term 'civil servant', even without any connection with his own career, he fell into a rage. I discovered that these outbursts of fury were, in a certain sense, still quarrels with his long-dead father, whose greatest desire it had been to turn him into a civil servant.

Kubizek remarks that Adolf was proud of his late father's position in society and used to speak of him with apparent respect. Adolf's mother would lament that her obstinate son would still not conform to paternal expectations: 'Your poor father cannot rest in his grave', she used to say to Adolf, 'because you do absolutely nothing that he wanted for you. Obedience is what distinguishes a good son, but you do not know the meaning of the word. That's why you did so badly at school and why you're not getting anywhere now.' Kubizek remarks that Adolf's dead father 'was still ever present to his family', adding with crucial insight: 'the authority of his father still remained, even after his death, the force in the struggle with which Adolf developed his own powers. His father's attitude had provoked him first to secret, then to open, rebellion.'

Kubizek rightly emphasises Adolf's continuing 'struggle' as being with his dead father. Alois had never settled and during his period of service in Braunau recorded twelve changes of address, often living in inns. He not only had three successive wives and several mistresses but also a total of nine children by them—he was certainly, unlike his son, sexually confident and very active. Unexpectedly, perhaps, Kubizek reports that Alois was 'inclined to liberal views' although fully submitting to the authority of the Austrian state and Emperor for whom he worked. What Kubizek means by 'liberal views' is not made obvious but, if he was referring to a free and easy sexuality, such a paternal trait may partly explain his son's subsequent sexual anxieties and lack of confidence; children can be intimidated by their parents' rampant sexuality.

Adolf's mother

Adolf states in *Mein Kampf*—'I had honoured my father, but my mother I loved'.

When we turn to consider Klara Hitler, Adolf's mother, the contrast with Alois is considerable. She was, in many ways, the opposite of her husband. Born Klara Pölzl in 1860 she was twenty-three years younger than Alois, and his second cousin, although addressing him as 'Uncle'. In 1876, aged sixteen, Klara had left the family farm and joined Uncle Alois in Braunau as his maid. Alois separated from his first wife in 1880 and his second died in 1884, by which time Klara was already pregnant by him. After receiving special dispensation on grounds of incest, the couple were married in January 1885. Three children were born in rapid succession but, by January 1888, all had died through illness. Then, on 20 April 1889, in a Gasthof where they were then living, Klara gave birth to Adolf, her first surviving child.

Kubizek, who met Klara Hitler often between 1904 and 1907 describes her as: 'a beautiful woman to the day of her death … submissive and accommodating … she told me once that Adolf was a very weak child and that she always lived in fear of losing him.' This fits with Paula Hitler's description of her mother as 'a very soft and tender person, the compensatory element between the almost too harsh father and the very lively children … '

Although her late husband's portrait hung upon the wall, Kubizek reports that Klara once confessed to him that 'what I hoped and dreamed of as a young girl has not been fulfilled in my marriage—but does such a thing ever happen?' Although he ignored her suggestions as regards his career, Adolf clearly adored his mother and she adored him. According to Ernst Hanfstaengl, a German-American associate of Hitler in the 1920s who later broke with him, Adolf once described himself as a milksop and a mother's boy (*muttersöhnchen*) and, according to Kubizek, by the age of eighteen, Adolf felt he ought to get away and become more independent of her. His mother was:

> the only person on earth to whom he felt really close … I was always surprised by the sympathetic understanding and patience with which Adolf tried to convince his mother of his artistic vocation. Contrary to his habit, he never became cross or violent on these occasions.

Klara remained anxious about Adolf, realising that he was lazy, unrealistic in his plans and without solid qualifications for a job or proper financial means of support. Early in 1907 she became ill and had an operation. Adolf visited her daily in hospital. When she had recovered Adolf finally left for Vienna intending to enter the Academy of Arts. Almost immediately his mother's breast cancer returned and Adolf came home to care for her, under the direction of the family's Jewish doctor, Dr Eduard Bloch. Kubizek recalls seeing Adolf shortly after Dr Bloch had broken the news to him of the seriousness of his mother's condition:

> He looked terrible. His face was so pale as to be almost transparent, his eyes were dull and his voice hoarse ... 'Incurable, the doctor says'—this was all he could utter ... his eyes blazed, his temper flared up. 'Incurable—what do they mean by that?' he screamed. 'Not that the malady is incurable, but that the doctors aren't capable of curing it. My mother isn't even old. Forty-seven isn't an age where you give up hope. But as soon as the doctors can't do anything, they call it incurable.'

The young Adolf now took over the running of his mother's cramped little household. Kubizek records:

> One day on my arrival at the Blütengasse I found Adolf kneeling on the floor. He was wearing a blue apron and scrubbing out the kitchen, which had not been cleaned for a long time. I was really immensely surprised and I must have shown it, for Frau Klara smiled in spite of her pain and said to me: '*There, you see, Adolf can do anything.*' [My emphasis] Then I noticed that Adolf had changed the furniture around. His mother's bed now stood in the kitchen because that was heated during the day. The kitchen cupboard had been moved into the living room, and in its place was the couch, on which Adolf slept, so that he could be near her during the night as well.

For the remaining weeks of his mother's life, eighteen-year-old Adolf, wearing his apron, did everything he could for her:

> Adolf anticipated her every wish and took the most tender care of her. I had never before seen in him such loving tenderness. I did not trust my own eyes and ears. Not a cross word, not an impatient remark, no violent insistence on having his own way. He forgot himself entirely in those weeks and lived only for his mother.

Adolf also had to care for his little sister Paula at this time and he made her swear to her mother that she would be a diligent and well-behaved pupil. Kubizek adds: 'Perhaps Adolf wanted to show his mother by this little scene that he had meanwhile realised his own faults.'

When Klara died just before Christmas (21 December), Adolf 'could hardly speak' yet made all the arrangements with the undertakers. Four days later it was Christmas Day but Adolf refused to visit either the Kubizeks or his half-sister Angela Raubal (he detested her civil servant husband), apparently spending it alone at the now empty home. In future years Christmas would always be a difficult season for Adolf, and in 1941, 1942 and 1944 he would make war-losing decisions at that time.

The US government's secret investigations of Adolf Hitler's character, directed by Walter Langer in 1943, would provide independent testimony to support Kubizek's. Langer interviewed Dr Bloch who had escaped shortly before the war: 'In all my career I have never seen anyone so prostrate with grief as Adolph Hitler', the doctor reported. Bloch was a kindly man but not necessarily a good practitioner. His treatment of Klara had possibly added to her pain. Yet Adolf never showed any anger towards him. Many have argued that this experience could have been the origin of Adolf's anti-semitism (which first appeared publicly twelve years later in 1919) but the young Adolf continued to send polite postcards to Bloch and did nothing to have him detained or punished when, in later years, he was in a position to do so.

Adolf

What was Adolf himself like as a boy? Sadly, except for his own accounts in *Mein Kampf*, and Kubizek's, we have very little to go on for the early years. Adolf has been described by Alan Bullock as a child who was

> self-willed and resistant to the discipline of regular work ... playing war games ... reading Karl May's adventure stories about the North American Indians ... his school

> reports continued to describe him as idle, wilful and disrespectful.

Ian Kershaw, similarly, sees little Adolf when a choirboy as 'intoxicated by the ecclesiastical splendour ... "a little ring-leader" in the game of cops and robbers which the village boys played in the woods and fields around their homes. War games were a particular favourite ... ' Kershaw quotes Adolf's class-teacher, Dr Eduard Huemer, as describing Adolf as a boy 'not making full use of his talent, lacking in application, and unable to accommodate himself to school discipline ... stubborn, high-handed, dogmatic and hot-tempered.'

Central to his development, says Kershaw, was his conflict with his aggressive father. Adolf turned into 'an idle, resentful, rebellious, sullen, stubborn and purposeless teenager.' He was, however, cosseted by his doting mother who believed he could 'do anything'. After his father's death, Kershaw says, Adolf

> lived a life of parasitic idleness ... during the days drawing, painting, reading or writing 'poetry'; the evenings were for going to the theatre or opera; and the whole time he day-dreamed and fantasized about his future as a great artist.

This is the point in his life, aged fifteen, when Adolf met August Kubizek. They were to spend much time together over the next four years, first in Linz and then in Vienna. Their relationship was fraternal and, indeed, Adolf would sometimes mistakenly address August Kubizek as 'Gustav' — the name of Adolf's mother's eldest son who had died before Adolf was born. Kubizek, in fact only nine months older, was from a similar background to Adolf and they had met, both solitary boys, while queuing for an opera. Kubizek was fascinated by young Adolf's quick, sure grasp and charisma, seeing him as — 'an artist who despised the mere bread-and-butter job and devoted himself to poetry, to drawing, painting and going to the theatre.'

Adolf said he did not trust adults in general nor their peculiar ideas, and accepted only his mother. 'He just had to talk and needed someone who would listen to him', says Kubizek, adding —

> everything aroused his (Adolf's) interest ... (he) had to find an outlet for his tempestuous feelings ... (he) seemed to be like a volcano erupting ... something strange, other-worldly, was bursting out of him ... such rapture ... this was not acting, not exaggeration, this was really felt ... how vividly he managed to convey his feelings, how easily the words flowed from his mouth.

This could be a classic description of *hypomania*—a psychiatric label used to describe abnormally elevated mood. (See Glossary.) Such a label would also fit with Adolf's outbursts of temper whenever thwarted or disagreed with, as well as with his sense of self-importance. Adolf, so Kubizek implies, was usually in this raised mood during his middle teens. The textbook criteria for a diagnosis of hypomania are a persistently elevated, expansive or irritable mood (for four or more days), decreased need for sleep, pressure of talk, inflated self-esteem or grandiosity, flight of ideas, distractibility, increased goal-directed behaviour and excessive involvement in pleasurable activities. Most of these traits fit Adolf Hitler very well, especially if one takes into account the exceptionally goal-directed behaviour of his later political career and the 'pleasurable activities' he was obsessed with—art, architecture, opera and music generally. He was always a poor sleeper, often staying awake until the early hours, and rising late. There is also a possible genetic correlation between mood disturbances and those, like Adolf, who sleep late and work best in the evenings. Perhaps an even better label for Adolf would be *cyclothymic*—a term used to describe persistent mood abnormality involving periods of both mild elation *and* mild depression—because depression later became an additional feature in Adolf's life. Whichever label is chosen, I am fairly certain that Adolf Hitler, by the age that Kubizek describes him, is already showing clear signs of a mild *bipolar mood disorder* of this sort. Any such condition is typically accompanied by marked impairments in social, occupational and sexual functioning—all of which also apply in Adolf's case. Studies show that an adolescent onset of bipolar disorder is associated with a family history of the condition—in Adolf's case, his father was probably also affected.

(We know of Alois' outbursts of temper and high levels of goal-directed behaviour.) Conditions of this sort are not particularly uncommon. Only if they become more severe —as in mania itself—are they likely to receive professional treatment, even today.

What else can Kubizek tell us of the young Adolf?

> He was never vain ... (he showed) a great likeness to his mother ... of middle height and slender ... not at all strong ... his health, in fact, was rather poor ... his eyes were so outstanding that one did not notice anything else ... they were the light eyes of his mother, but her somewhat staring penetrating gaze was even more marked ... his sonorous voice ... extraordinary eloquence ... his language was very refined ... he disliked dialect ... Adolf had shown a gift for oratory from his earliest youth, and he knew it ... (he soared) high in his fantasies ... there was nothing that Hitler could not achieve by a convincing speech.

Unusually, perhaps, for those who experience sustained elevations of mood, the 'know it all' Adolf was also a shy, controlled and 'obsessoid' boy: he 'set great store by good manners ... a faultless crease (in his trousers) ... a well groomed appearance ... professional success was not at all his ambition.'

Kubizek goes on to describe Adolf as a romantic loner with:

> ... undoubted histrionic talents ... details did not interest him ... contempt for everything pertaining to the body—sport ... meant nothing to him ... his love of Nature was pronounced ... he did feel at home with nature ... being outdoors had an extraordinary effect on him ... then (he became) quite a different person ... there he would read his books, sketch and paint in watercolours ... his first poems ... give full reign to his imagination ... an open air study (where he could) cultivate undisturbed his passionate plans and ideas.

Adolf was obsessed with buildings and was constantly planning new living spaces, bridges, stations and museums. He also planned plays and endlessly discussed with Kubizek the operas they had seen together. Kubizek had genuine musical skills and could more than keep up on this front. Richard Wagner, Franz Lehar and Anton Bruckner were their favourite composers. Adolf was always somewhat inscrutable, Kubizek says, but when faced with great art, fired by 'his enthusiasm for beauty', he would lower his defences. Adolf, however, was 'a deeply serious man' ... who showed a 'deadly earnestness ... (he) never ceased to attack new problems ... a carefree letting-go of himself ... was alien to him'.

Yet, and here the stereotype of Adolf Hitler suffers a further blow, Adolf was, so Kubizek writes:

> full of deep understanding and sympathy ... he knew exactly how I felt ... he always knew what I needed ... however intensely he was occupied with himself he would always have time for the affairs of those people in whom he was interested.

Once he rescued Kubizek's mother when she fell in the water: 'He always remained attached to my parents. As late as 1944, on my mother's 80th birthday, he sent her a food parcel.'

Kubizek joined Adolf in Vienna in 1907 where, full of confidence, Adolf applied for entrance to the Academy of Arts. Only twenty-eight candidates out of approximately eighty were accepted and Adolf was not among them. 'Test drawing unsatisfactory. Few heads,' was the verdict of the examiners. With remarkable candour Adolf described this rebuff in *Mein Kampf*:

> I was so convinced that I would be successful that when I received my rejection, it struck me as a bolt from the blue. Yet that is what happened. When I presented myself to the rector, requesting an explanation for my non-acceptance at the Academy's school of painting, that gentleman assured me that the drawings I had submitted incontrovertibly showed my unfitness for painting, and that my ability obviously lay in the field of architecture ... In a few days I myself knew that I should some day become an architect.

Contrary to the usual contempt expressed for *Mein Kampf* I find this passage refreshingly honest. Adolf's principal dream had been shattered but, accepting advice, he simply reconfigured it. Architecture, and not art, would now be his goal. He would spend the remainder of his life planning the future architecture of an all-powerful Germany. Indeed,

Kubizek claims that Adolf later saw the Second World War as a tiresome interlude and reports that, after their happy reunion in 1938, Adolf invited him to the performance of Wagner's *Götterdämmerung* at Bayreuth in 1940 saying to him, at that event, in 'a growling undertone'—'This war will set us back many years in our building programme. It is a tragedy. I did not become Chancellor of the Greater German Reich to fight wars.' Even during the war years Adolf would spend hours with his protégé Albert Speer discussing their futuristic building plans for the Reich while his desperate generals were forced to wait outside.

Speer—the young man with the architectural skills and status that Adolf himself would have liked to have—became the closest of his top-ranking wartime colleagues after Rudolf Hess had flown off to Britain in 1941. The plans themselves were spectacular—order and sheer size dominating the designs for the new Berlin.

After his mother's death in December 1906 Adolf eventually returned to Vienna. He tried again to enter the Academy of Arts but again failed. He had not told his dying mother of his first failure and now, initially at least, he concealed both rejections from his only friend August Kubizek, with whom he was sharing his lodgings.

Kubizek says:

> Nothing more terrible could have happened to him. But he was too proud to talk about it, and so concealed from me what had occurred ... he did not mention it at all ... There was neither revolt nor rebellion, instead came a radical withdrawal into himself.

So Adolf had suffered two huge losses within twelve months—the death of his beloved mother and the double failure to be accepted by the Academy of Arts. For such a youth—romantic, narcissistic, lonely and self-important—these blows must have been psychologically devastating. Biographers often describe the next seven years of degradation as if they had no explanation, yet I think they indicate, quite simply, that Adolf became significantly depressed as a reaction to these blows. What was his behaviour like at this time? Kubizek says:

> ... in these early days in Vienna, I had the impression that Adolf had become unbalanced. He would fly into a temper at the slightest thing. There were days when nothing I could do seemed right to him, and he made our life together very hard to bear ... I did not know what this present mood of deep depression was due to, but I thought that sooner or later it would improve ... Wherever he looked, he saw injustice, hate and enmity. Nothing was free from his criticism, nothing found favour in his eyes.

Clearly Adolf was trying to turn his anger outwards, away from himself and onto the world. He was trying, sometimes unsuccessfully, to find a scapegoat for his misery:

> He wallowed deeper and deeper in self-criticism. Yet it only needed the lightest touch—as when one flicks on the light and everything becomes brilliantly clear—for his self-accusation to become an accusation against the times, against the whole world. Choking with his catalogue of hates, he would pour his fury over everything, against mankind in general who did not understand him, who did not appreciate him and by whom he was persecuted.

As his father was dead, whom could he blame? In these years Adolf would stay in bed in the mornings (as unemployed depressives often do) and spend much of the night poring over his architectural designs and writings. Eventually, Adolf admitted to Kubizek that the Academy had rejected him and attacked the institution's examiners in words that suggest he saw them as being like his father: 'This Academy is a lot of old-fashioned fossilised civil servants, bureaucrats, devoid of understanding, stupid lumps of officials. The whole Academy ought to be blown up!'

At this time, according to Kubizek, Adolf developed 'a demoniacal hatred of that unearned wealth, presumptuous and arrogant, which we saw around us'. Yet he kept up his appearances. 'No-one meeting this carefully dressed young man in the street would have thought that he went hungry everyday ... ' It is in this period, surely, that his personal experience of life paved the way for his Socialism. He began to detest property speculators, exploitative landlords and the squalid housing of the Viennese working class. He started to plan gardens, playgrounds for children, railways, better water supplies, drains, bathrooms, and light and airy houses. 'I am working on the solution of the housing problem in Vienna', he announced. Houses had become more real to him than people. With his usual insight Kubizek remarks: 'No doubt this ardent desire for a total reorganisation of life was his personal response to his own fate.' He was certainly trying to reorganise and re-plan himself but was he also, unconsciously, planning a better living space for his dead mother? It was what she had always wanted.

Adolf became obsessionally clean in these years of misery and hygiene mattered a great deal to him. Kubizek refers to his 'constant fear of physical contact with strangers—he shook hands only rarely and then only with a few people'. This may reflect an underlying fear of sexual contact. He was becoming paranoid too. He now told Kubizek that the Academy had *deliberately* contrived to fail him. 'He spoke of the trip-wires which had been cunningly laid—I remember his very words—for the sole purpose of ruining his career ... there was a great conspiracy against him—he had no possibility of earning any money.'

He never showed any interest in meeting others with specialised knowledge of the subjects that enthralled him. Instead he would sit alone on a bench in the park and discuss such matters with himself. His private world was his escape.

After his mother's demise Adolf had inherited a small amount of money but insufficient for his needs in Vienna. Gradually he sank down the social ladder until, after spending the summer of 1909 sleeping on park benches, and moving from lodging to lodging, he managed to find a place in a refuge for the homeless. He had no job, but would spend his days reading and sometimes talking grandiosely to the other drop-outs. Then, perhaps with financial help from his mother's sister, he moved into a working men's hostel where he sat in the canteen for much of the day. An associate in those 'wilderness years', after Adolf had lost touch with Kubizek in 1908, was Reinhold Hanisch who sold a few of Adolf's postcard-sized paintings for him. Significantly perhaps, Hanisch describes the thin little Adolf at this age as 'looking Jewish'. But Hanisch eventually lost his patience with the down-and-out Adolf over his 'idleness'. (This idleness was, I would suggest, a natural trait intensified by his depression.) Nevertheless, occasionally, Adolf could still find sufficient of his old energy to lecture Hanisch on the beauties of Wagner and of certain of the buildings in Vienna. Another acquaintance, and of a similar name, Karl Honisch, knew Adolf in Vienna in 1913 and, in the 1930s, wrote a eulogistic account of him for the Nazi archive, depicting Adolf as being rarely absent from the hostel, sitting always at the same place at the long oak table, drawing and painting, keeping his physical distance from others and, occasionally, hot-headedly and eloquently, joining in discussions with the other inmates.

In 1913 Adolf moved to Munich, registering himself as stateless and, after months of evading conscription, eventually enlisted in the German army in August 1914 on the eve of the Great War. In the four years that followed, Adolf at last found some sense of purpose and structure in his life. He even won a medal, on the recommendation of a Jewish officer, for rescuing a wounded comrade. Regarded as rather odd by his fellow soldiers his only close companion for some months was a dog he adopted, and Adolf was bitterly upset when this animal was later stolen from him. When the war ended, the gassed and wounded Adolf felt betrayed. No sooner had he found a meaning to his life than it had been dashed from him! He had been stationed on parts of the front that had not seen many German defeats and he could hardly believe that the Allies deserved their victory. Angry and rebellious, he became increasingly politicised, nationalistic and, apparently for the first time, anti-semitic. In October 1918, just before the armistice, Adolf had been blinded after an Allied gas attack and was admitted for treatment at Pasework where, according to the British psychologist David Lewis writing in 2003, a German neurologist, Dr Edmund Forster, had secretly diagnosed the blindness as being hysterical in origin. At the time, such a diagnosis would have been highly pejorative and could have been seen as tantamount to cowardice, a charge on which hundreds of soldiers had been tried and shot.

Forster, however, assured Adolf that the cause of the blindness was physical and told him that he (Adolf) was an exceptional man, chosen by God, who could use his extraordinary and heaven-sent will-power as a cure. This treatment worked but, according to Lewis, it also confirmed and intensified Adolf's already established belief in his messianic specialness and mission. This account, so it seems to me, also suggests an additional reason for Adolf's strange insistence upon waging an apparently unnecessary war in 1939; it was as if he was still continuing the Great War of 1918 in an effort to deny and 'cancel out' his own unconscious cowardice. He may still have felt huge, narcissistically exaggerated, guilt for Germany's defeat some twenty years earlier.

Walter Langer's report

In 1943 Walter Langer, a leading American psychoanalyst, was ordered by the Office of Strategic Studies to set up a team of experts to make a secret psychological study of Adolf Hitler for political and military purposes. The resultant report, eventually to be entitled *The Secret Mind of Adolf Hitler*, is a remarkable and pioneering work of psycho-biography. Langer's evidence came chiefly from interviews with about a dozen people who had met Adolf, and from *Mein Kampf* itself. (Langer had neither the Kubizek nor Junge first-hand accounts nor, of course, the great post-war biographies. He would, I suppose, have encountered Krueger's book.)

Langer describes the almost religious nature of the Nazi movement and the worship of its leader, seen by many Germans as a Christ-like figure. His witnesses describe Adolf in the 1920s and 1930s as working for days with little or no sleep and impatient to get things done. Yet he was often considerate towards his junior staff. Adolf deliberately took trouble, as he admits in *Mein Kampf*, to attract the political support of the marginalised in German society – the lower classes, women and young people, and give to them a clear emotive message. Yet Adolf himself suffered from 'an all-embracing disorderliness'. He was often 'on the go but rarely on time' and unable to maintain any kind of working schedule. He stayed awake at night but, contrary to the propaganda, not working, but watching films, listening to music or talking to his staff. He would often procrastinate, deferring decisions until his 'inner voice' told him what to do. Adolf's humour was mostly limited to teasing his colleagues. Langer quotes Friedelinde Wagner, who recalled Adolf once saying:

> You know what a volt is and an ampere, don't you? Right. But do you know what a goebbels and a goering are? A goebbels is the amount of nonsense a man can speak in an hour and a goering is the amount of metal that can be pinned on a man's chest.

(Adolf is here referring to his propaganda chief Joseph Goebbels, and to his absurdly vain and over-decorated henchman Hermann Goering.)

It is interesting to note that reports of Adolf's humour usually come from women and not from men. His jokes are *about* men but told to women. Adolf would also mimic male visitors such as the British Ambassador and Neville Chamberlain. He is still the rebellious child, siding with his mother and mocking his father.

Langer considered that Adolf's women friends fell into three categories—older women, passing fancies such as actresses, and more enduring relationships. Adolf would put up with quite a lot of criticism and scoldings from the former group which included various 'foster mothers' such as Helena Bechstein, Victoria von Dirksen, Winifred Wagner and Heinrich Hoffman's wife. According to Dr Eduard Bloch, so Langer relates, Adolf's mother was 'a very quiet, sweet, and affectionate woman whose life centred around her children and particularly Adolf, who was her pet'. Adolph's older half-brother, Alois junior, heartily disliked Adolf, feeling that Klara spoiled him. This view was shared, apparently, by Adolf's 'decent and industrious' half-sister Angela Raubal. Adolf's mother, says Langer, was neat, orderly and devout. She pampered and overprotected Adolf who was the apple of her eye. He remained so, despite the arrival of two younger siblings and became increasingly her pet after one of these, Edmund, died in 1900. At school, says Langer, the other boys were not greatly impressed by Adolf and his 'big-talk'. Adolf was lazy and uncooperative and lived in a world of fantasy. When twelve, Adolf may have been in trouble for some sexual misdemeanour with a little girl, but the evidence is not clear.

Adolf found the First World War 'like a redemption from the vexatious experiences of my youth'. During these years Adolf went out of his way to be subservient to his superior officers and was not popular with the other men. After the war Adolf suffered from nightmares. These were possibly signs of post traumatic stress and would have been found in many survivors from the trenches. Yet, according to Langer, one of his witnesses had heard that, on one occasion, the half-asleep Adolf had been found 'swaying in his room, looking wildly about him. "He! He! He's been here!" he gasped. His lips were blue. Sweat streamed down his face ... then suddenly he broke out "There, there! In the corner! Who's that?"' These are not typical of the nightmares of war and suggest a deep fear of an individual — perhaps, in Adolf's case, his father.

Langer unwittingly produces further evidence for believing that Adolf was bipolar. What had happened, he asked, 'to transform the lazy Vienna beggar into the energetic politician who never seemed to tire from rushing from one meeting to another and who was able to work thousands of listeners into a state of frenzy?' Strangely, Langer can find no rational explanation, yet mood change seems to me to be the obvious explanation.

Rightly, Langer goes through *Mein Kampf* with a toothcomb and finds much of psychological importance in Adolf's childhood that reverberates in his later life. As Adolf himself admits, when speaking of the memories of a boy of three—'In many intelligent people, traces of these early memories are found even in old age'. Adolf goes on to tell a crucially important story:

> Let us imagine the following: in a basement apartment of two stuffy rooms live a worker's family ... Among the five children there is a boy, let us say, of three. The smallness and overcrowding of the rooms do not create favourable conditions. Quarrelling and nagging often arise because of this. When the parents fight almost daily, their brutality leaves nothing to the imagination ... especially when the mutual differences express themselves in the form of brutal attacks on the part of the father towards the mother or to assaults due to drunkenness. The poor little boy, at the age of six, senses things which would make even a grown-up shudder. Morally infected, the young 'citizen' wanders off to elementary school.

What, exactly, was the 'moral infection' suffered by the little boy in Adolf's story? Could it be sexual arousal stimulated by seeing his mother being sexually abused?

I agree with Langer that, however it is disguised, this highly significant passage is Adolf recalling his own childhood. Although Adolf's father would, while sober, appear to be 'the soul of dignity', when drunk he became 'brutal, unjust and inconsiderate', hitting his wife, his children and his dog. Later Adolf admits witnessing 'with disgust and indignation' lower class families where 'the wife, for the sake of the children, stands up against ... (the) drunk and brutal (husband)'. Although Langer, in my opinion, rightly recognises Adolf's great anger towards his father he does not go on, as I do, to see Adolf's hatred of the Jews and, indeed, the waging of the war itself, as expressions of this anger. Adolf was, says Langer, so afraid of his aggressive fantasies being discovered by his father that he repressed them. Adolf feared his father's retaliation might entail his 'castration', says Langer, and this is the origin of Adolf's constant fears of death and of syphilis, and of his sexual impotence. Langer also suspects that Adolf's thwarted sexuality had become 'diffused' so that he became obsessed with eyes (and looking at pornography), with faeces, with buttocks, with mouths (and so with creamy cakes and his own oratory). Adolf also tried to idealise women by removing any taint of sexuality from them. In general, Langer sees Adolf's problems as Oedipal (see Glossary), and detects a strongly negative component in Adolf's feelings for his mother, suspecting that Adolf was angry with her for submitting to her husband and for her 'disloyalty' to Adolf in doing so: 'he hated his father for his brutality, he distrusted his mother for her lack of loyalty, and despised himself for his weakness'.

In my opinion Langer gets a little too carried away by psychoanalytic theory when he speculates about Adolf's sex life and its importance to Adolf's whole career. Otto Strasser apparently admitted to Langer that he had had an affair with Geli Raubal, Adolf's beloved niece, and that Geli had confessed to him not only that she was having sex with Adolf but that her uncle would persuade her to squat over his face and urinate upon him (undinism). Langer also reports what is little more than a rumour, that an actress, Renate Mueller, had confessed that a naked Adolf had lain upon the floor and implored her to kick him, condemning himself loudly as being unworthy even to be in the same room with her. Langer, probably correctly, sees these behaviours as masochistic. However, he also goes on to call them 'coprophagic' (faeces-eating). As soon as Adolf feels warm feelings for a woman, says Langer, 'he feels compelled to degrade himself in the eyes of the loved object and eat their dirt figuratively, if not literally'. Actually, there is no evidence for literal coprophagea, and there is a great difference between a sexual interest in urination and a desire to eat faeces. The former is a common condition while the latter is rare. Rightly, I think, Langer sees Adolf as identifying, to an unusual degree, with his mother who was, says Langer, also masochistic. Strangely, Langer does not look in any detail at the other side of such masochistic sexual behaviour—its potential sadism. Often the two sides co-exist. Was Adolf also sadistic towards his relatively few sexual partners? Is this why four or five of them committed or attempted suicide? Followers of Langer have suggested it was the coprophagea or undinism that drove them to such desperation. But it could have been his sadism that did so. Would such sadism also help to explain Adolf's cruel policies?

Langer also raises the possibility that Adolf felt both joy and guilt at the deaths of his brother and father which occurred more or less at the same time in his childhood. Adolf, who may have wished them dead, may have fantasised that his thoughts had actually killed them. In young minds such fantasies do indeed occur sometimes, and may have reinforced in Adolf his belief that he possessed special powers of a supernatural origin and that his survival (while others around him died) was ordained by Providence.

Finally, Langer suggests that Adolf was disgusted by his own coprophagic sexual perversion and projected this feeling onto the Jews. Thus, when warning against Jewish domination Adolf was defending himself from 'being dominated by his own perversion'. Adolf hated the 'dirty' Jews as much as he unconsciously hated himself. Langer concludes that Adolf was impotent but not homosexual. Crucially, Adolf was haunted by 'an extreme form of masochism in which the individual derives sexual gratification from the act of having a woman urinate or defecate on him'. Langer's central theory—that Hitler's disgust at this masochistic and coprophagic sexual perversion was the driving force for his anti-semitism and even, perhaps, for his whole political career—is tantalising. The evidence, however, is not exactly overwhelming and, even if true, it can only be *part* of the answer.

Kurt Kreuger's book

After reading the recent biographies and formulating my own psychological views of Adolf, I discovered a curious book that had been published in New York in 1941 by a Kurt Kreuger who claimed to have been Hitler's doctor in Munich between 1919 and 1934. Kreuger apparently had been a non-Jewish Nazi sympathiser but had eventually thought it wise to flee to America. Historians have cast some doubt upon this book's authenticity but it is probably written by someone who knew Adolf well. It purports to describe some fifteen years of 'psychoanalysis' with Hitler, allegedly as treatment for his impotence. If this is true,

Krueger would not meet the standards of orthodox psychoanalysis today. He hectors and directs his patient far too aggressively, unprofessionally disapproving of Adolf's alleged latent homosexuality while clearly sharing his anti-semitism. At the least, this appears to be a heavily embroidered report. Without clinical notes how could any therapist recall long passages of dialogue that allegedly occurred six or more years before the book's publication? Nevertheless, there are glimpses of Adolf that are almost certainly genuine. Krueger describes, for example, Adolf's alternating moods of 'despair' and 'exuberance', and his obvious childhood closeness with his mother. He concludes, predictably, that all Adolf's problems are due to this Oedipus complex. What are particularly intriguing are Krueger's allegations that Adolf had indulged in sadistic sexual practices with women, had been cruel to an animal (a mouse) in his childhood, suffered from vertigo, had been seduced by Ernst Roehm (whom he later ordered to be shot), had masochistic erotic fantasies and had murdered Geli Raubal in a jealous rage. His affair with Geli apparently began after he caught her in flagrante with his chauffeur. Adolf spanked her and was swept by 'an emotional hurricane'. In bed with her his 'violent passion' was suddenly overcome by a brief delusion that she was his mother—'her flesh became too sacred to be possessed ... it was as if she were struggling to remain a harlot while I wanted her to resume the role of angel ...' Adolf allegedly confesses to Krueger his deep guilt over Geli's death and complains of nightmares in which Geli appears to him streaming with blood. If genuine, this is hugely rich material. Before Geli's death there had been other nightmares too, and Adolf allegedly complained to Krueger of insomnia and sleepwalking. The content, however, of these older nocturnal fears are never identified by Krueger.

Krueger reports many other interesting behaviours. Every afternoon at 2pm precisely, as if hearing his mother's alarm clock in his head, says Krueger, Adolf felt compelled to have a bath. He alleges that Adolf used to sleep in his parents' bed until the age of ten, longing to be close to his mother and resenting the presence of his naked father. Occasionally, when his father was away, Adolf would sleep alone with his mother. Two young men appear as possible lovers of his mother, one a Jewish neighbour called Sachs. Adolf had felt jealous of them and once, allegedly, saw Sachs fondling his mother's naked breasts; the little Adolf had then vomited. Adolf admitted that he believed, as a child, that his father loved his mother but that his mother really loved him (Adolf). Adolf used to cry for 'the hypothetical father whom I should have had' but he apparently never admits to Krueger that his father used to beat him; although he claims his mother did and he enjoyed it. Nevertheless, Adolf admits to his 'supreme hatred' of his father and to a fantasy of rescuing his mother from his father's clutches. Adolf allegedly recalled children in the neighbourhood jeering at his father and himself as Jews. Indeed, Adolf himself had once called Alois a Jew to his face. If true, these reports are all highly important.

Krueger mentions that Adolf had two possible reasons to suspect his own partial Jewishness; either because Alois was half Jewish or because Sachs was his real father. He also describes Adolf's messianic complex. Adolf apparently tells Krueger that he concurs with Schopenhauer that 'Satan, the Jew and the sex organ are one, all one and the same thing'. Krueger concludes that Adolf is terrified of his homosexuality, and is 'a terribly lonely, frustrated man, followed wherever he goes by his fear and distrust of women, his loathing of a people he has good reason to believe are his own flesh and blood'. Yet, it is clear that Adolf did make progress in liberating his sexuality. The prim virgin of the Vienna days gradually matured into a more relaxed man who could talk frankly about the attraction he felt for teenage girls. Eventually he could make jokes about the sex lives of his colleagues and even his own. His natural affection for women and his ability to enjoy some sort of sexuality with them finally come together in his relationship with Eva Braun. Maybe Kreuger's peculiar psychoanalysis, if it occurred, was not entirely the failure Krueger thought it was.

We should not be so prejudiced against the Nazi-sympathising Krueger that we reject out of hand his account as being necessarily untrue, nor merely because we remain unsure of his identity. Could he have been just who he claimed to be—Hitler's doctor? Despite the new 'facts', there is little in his account that clashes with my own psychological interpretation, nor with that of Walter Langer. Indeed, if true, it remarkably strengthens the conclusions I had already reached before I discovered Krueger's strange book. In a foreword, the prominent Nazi exile, Otto Strasser, one of Hitler's most deadly and resourceful enemies, mentions that Adolf used to pester his niece Geli for sexual favours and locked her up when she refused; he was tremendously possessive of her, keeping her away from other men. Adolf became deeply depressed after he allegedly shot Geli, and Strasser claims he had to prevent Adolf from committing suicide at that time.

Despite the identity of Krueger being uncertain it is beyond doubt that this book was first published in New York in 1941 under the title *Inside Hitler*, with a foreword by Upton Sinclair. The mildly absurd ambiguity of its initial title in English (which was rapidly changed) suggests it really is the creation of a German-speaker and not the work of Allied Intelligence. Beyond that it remains a mystery. I report its contents not because they are undoubtedly true but because they might be. If they are, they strongly support my central thesis—a thesis developed, however, before I had read Kreuger's book.

Adolf's sex life

What, then, of Adolf's sexuality? Have post-war studies revealed any more reliable information on this topic? Apparently Adolf once confided in Hanisch that a milk-maid had made advances to him when he was a schoolboy and, frightened, he had knocked over her milk-churn as he ran away. Hanisch concluded that Adolf had 'very austere ideas about relations between men and women'. Walter Langer, as we have seen, attached a great deal of importance to Adolf's sex-life in his wartime analysis, finding that Adolf had a masochistic perversion in persuading his niece Geli Raubal, seventeen years his junior, to squat over his face and urinate on him. Today, such a practice might not appear to be of such great psychological importance but in 1930s Germany it may indeed have had some of the significance that Langer attributed to it. Some have queried the authenticity of the story because the source for this information was Strasser who had every reason to want to discredit Hitler. Nevertheless, Adolf was deeply fascinated by Geli and did, almost certainly, have some sort of sexual relationship with her, and one probably tinged with sado-masochism. It is significant, surely, that Geli called him 'Uncle' just as his mother had addressed his father, and had been, like Klara with Alois, Adolf's live-in servant.

Furthermore, Geli (who was his half-sister Angela Raubal's daughter) had been born the night before Adolf's mother had died at Christmas in 1907. In other words she must have been very much associated in Adolf's mind with his own childhood and with his mother. An additional reason, however, why Adolf fell for Geli was that, being her uncle and aged thirty-five, he felt sufficiently in a position of power over the eighteen year old to allow his sexual feelings to have natural and confident expression. Most of his genuine sexual relationships with women were of this dominant type—he preferred shop-girls or typists who were in their teens. As regards both their social standing and their age he could feel their superior, and this gave him the confidence to overcome his basic feelings of sexual inadequacy. There was also an element of familial repetition here and, as Michael Hession has pointed out, the servant-master type of sexual relationship may extend back at least three generations: Geli with Adolf, Klara with Alois, and, possibly, Maria Anna Schiklgruber with her unknown lover.

Adolf may not have had sex-appeal but he did have verbal charisma, celebrity and growing political power and these three qualities attracted quite a few women to him over the years, although it seems that he very rarely took full advantage of this in sexual terms. Why not? Well, he was certainly shy, and he also feared physical contact, dirt and disease, and perhaps, was not particularly highly sexed anyway. It is also possible to argue along psychoanalytic lines that he felt unconscious Oedipal guilt about sex, having been very close to his mother. In his earlier years, at least, he appeared to see women as too pure for physical sexuality but not to be trusted in matters of love. Equally compelling, his diatribe about syphilis in *Mein Kampf* suggests that he had either caught the disease (perhaps from a prostitute in Vienna) or at least *feared* that he had done so. His quack doctor, appointed in later years, Dr Theodor Morell, who was to poison Adolf's brain with amphetamines and many other drugs during the 1940s, had been something of a syphilis specialist. Adolf certainly had strange ideas about sex. He felt that in 1930s Germany people were getting married not because they loved each other, but for social and financial reasons. (Did he fantasise that his mother had done this?) He seemed to believe that this would produce weaker children. (Himself?) For similar reasons he advocated early marriage; it would produce healthy and resistant offspring. Weak people were vulnerable to the 'Jewish disease' of Marxism. Syphilis begins to seek its victims among fourteen and fifteen year olds, so Adolf warned, caught from 'big-city whores' and the 'moral plague of big-city "civilisation"'. This is Adolf at his most confused. Sex, syphilis, Marxism, prostitution, moral degradation, and Jewishness all became mixed up in his mind; all are symptoms, he thought, of 'a slowly rotting world'. This is surely an externalised view of his own, as he felt it, inner rottenness, although it is impossible to be sure that this refers, as Langer would have it, to his disgust with his own masochistic and coprophagic perversion. It is typical of the ideation that depressives sometimes project, in a paranoid manner, onto the external world. As is usual in such cases, the full-blown paranoid system, in his case anti-semitism, does not take firm root in his mind until he is in his thirties.

One of Kubizek's most interesting (and most disbelieved) revelations is that, for years, the teenage Hitler had entertained the fantasy that he was in love with a young woman in Linz named Stephanie Izak and that she was in love with him. In fact she hardly knew him and had no idea of his feelings for her. Yet, for years, Stephanie became a talisman for the lonely Adolf—an icon of romanticised love and unblemished beauty. This was the pure and loving relationship that part of him yearned for. Kubizek says that Adolf never actually had a sexual relationship in Linz or Vienna and that he had a 'strict moral attitude' towards such matters. (This is consistent with the later opinion of Rheinhold Hanisch.) Adolf probably preferred a fantasy Stephanie to risking any actual 'disloyalty', as he may have unconsciously construed it, towards his mother; or perhaps his fear of sex was based upon his terror of being 'betrayed' or abandoned by a woman. Whenever the subjects of sex, love or marriage were raised, says Kubizek, Adolf would mysteriously murmur—'the flame of life'. He had to keep this flame pure, whatever he meant by it. Increasingly, one begins to realise how important Adolf's sexual dysfunction may have been in the development of his later political career. His early sexual frustration, guilt and disgust, whatever their origin, surely augmented his hatred of the world. According to Kubizek, Adolf one night suggested that they visit the red-light district of Vienna—'Come, Gustl, we must see the sink of iniquity once'. They walked down the street full of brothels looking in on the scantily clad girls in the illuminated windows. At the end of the street Adolf turned around and they walked back again. 'Adolf grew angry at the prostitutes' tricks of seduction', Kubizek recalls, saying that 'the girls in question thought only of their earnings' and that 'in practice the flame of life in these poor creatures was long since extinct'. Was Adolf referring to his idea of 'true love' and, perhaps, to his mother's love for him? He feared that a woman's love would lack sincerity and trust. Did he unconsciously feel a similar ambivalence towards his mother? Kubizek states that he believed that Adolf even refrained from masturbation at this time. He wanted to avoid 'infection ... by the vortex of corruption ...

he remained a man alone and—an odd contradiction—in strict monk-like asceticism guarded the holy flame of life.'

In Sayer and Botting's opinion, Adolf believed that he brought disaster to women. This idea was encouraged when Adolf's first real girlfriend, Maria Reiter, tried to commit suicide in 1926. A shop assistant, Maria (or Mimi as she preferred to be called) had one day caught sight of Adolf and his Alsatian dog Prinz shortly after his release from prison (following his unsuccessful coup of 1923), when she was only sixteen and he was thirty-seven. 'My mother had the same eyes as you' Adolf later told her. 'She died when I was young, like you.' Mimi's mother, too, had just died of cancer. So with both Mimi and Geli the links with his mother were clearly in his mind. If reports are true, Mimi's birthday (23 December) was also, like Geli's, the day on which Klara Hitler had been buried. When Adolf had first asked Mimi for a kiss she had refused. 'Then we shall never see each other again!' he had cried dramatically, dashing from the room. A few days later she allowed him the kiss and they saw each other on many occasions over the next few months, Adolf eventually declaring his love for her. When senior members of the new Nazi party discovered the relationship they insisted that Adolf put an end to it, fearing that the age-difference would create a scandal. The jilted Mimi put a length of cord around her neck and half-strangled herself. After the war Mimi claimed, in an article in Stern Magazine, that they had eventually become 'true lovers—in every sense of the word' and Paula Hitler, Adolf's little sister, was reported to have told Mimi—'I believe if he had married you, history might have been different.'

According to Sayer and Botting, more than half a dozen of Adolf's lady friends were eventually to attempt or succeed in suicide, the most well known of whom was the disturbed and sexually unattractive Unity Mitford. Eva Braun would try twice. Although some of Sayer and Botting's sources are not as validated as historians would prefer, they tell a fairly consistent and convincing story of a heterosexual Adolf who clearly lacked sexual confidence. Rampant sexuality was something he may have associated with his hated father—and consequently despised. Perhaps he also unconsciously feared 'castration'—that is to say, some kind of punitive violence against his sexuality from the internalised presence of his father. Frequently he used, as a reason for not marrying, the excuse that he had to put Germany's interests first. This sounded good but was it the real reason? A mother's boy often has a problem with women in later life; he desperately *needs* motherly love but does not *want* it. Maybe, as psychoanalysts insist, this is due to Oedipal feelings either over 'betraying the mother' or because sexuality stirs up guilt and disgust associated with unconscious sexual longings for the mother. Perhaps, if he saw Germany as his mother, then Adolf did speak the truth, and he was indeed being loyal to her. Oedipal or not, there is often a simple fear in such men that involvement with a woman will cause them to lose their freedom and sense of identity. Being fussed and 'spoiled' by a mother often deeply threatens the identity-formation of the child and they can fight back with a passion for liberty and independence, as indeed Adolf did. Some, like Adolf, become obstinate loners, rigidly sticking to their own ideas, and escaping into a world of make-believe.

I do not consider that sexuality is always of paramount importance in personality development but in Adolf's case it certainly had some significance. In his book Kurt Krueger claimed that 'a somewhat dishevelled' ex-soldier presented himself to him in August 1919, 'with a pair of wild suffering eyes and lonely and secret pain … his shattered nerves driving him to an eternal combat with himself, which he mistook for the hostility of the world … ' Adolf Hitler, if it was he, said he had syphilis. Krueger examined him and found no sign of the disease. '"But if I haven't got syphilis", my patient insisted, "how is it that I am totally impotent?"' Fears and delusions of illness, and particularly of sexual infection, are not only common, but frequently found in the anxious and depressed. Impotence, too, is often psychologically caused and is far from uncommon in battle-shattered men. Anxiety about impotence itself increases the condition so that it can become a vicious circle. We simply do not know if this report is true, but if Krueger's account is accurate, it does provide another piece in the jigsaw of understanding Adolf. If Adolf really was impotent, or at least *feared* that he was, this would not only affect his relationship with women, it could shatter his confidence generally. It might even have been a reason why Adolf, already convinced of his genius and destiny, turned to politics and violence after the First War as ways of asserting the potency that he felt he otherwise lacked. It was at this time, too, just after the defeat of Germany, that Adolf starts to announce publicly his anti-semitism.

In September 1930, after four years of sharing his flat in Munich, Geli apparently found a letter from a new and younger girlfriend, Eva Braun, in the pocket of one of Uncle Adolf's jackets. Uncle and niece had a row and, when Adolf left to visit Hamburg, Geli most likely went to her bedroom and shot herself with Adolf's 6.35mm pistol. (Krueger, as we have seen, claims it was Adolf who pulled the trigger.) According to his photographer, Heinrich Hoffmann, Adolf was entirely inconsolable—'Geli's death had shaken my friend to the depths of his soul ... his face was grey with anguish ... ' It may have been a political spur to Adolf. Hoffmann reports that almost the first words uttered by Adolf after Geli's death were, 'So, now let the struggle begin ...' Once again it is that word 'struggle'. What exactly did he mean? Geli's death was, like his mother's, a mortifying blow. A woman, whom he associated with his mother, had, once more, shattered and rejected him through death. But where did Adolf put the blame? Onto himself? Onto the woman? Or, once again, onto the external world against which he had to 'struggle'? In later years Adolf was to see suicide as an honourable way out when faced by defeat. For many years Adolf was to carry a photograph of Geli, together with one of his mother, in his pocket. Significantly, every Christmas—the anniversary of his mother's death and Geli's birthday—Adolf would go to Geli's bedroom to remember them and keep vigil. Ernst Hanfstaengl believed that Geli was a woman who might have brought him relief, defusing the fires of anger within him and, possibly, drawing off his sado- masochistic tendencies. 'Here was this man with a volcanic store of energy, with no apparent outlet except his almost medium-like performances on a speaker's platform.' Hanfstaengl was not the only acquaintance who was to make such a point. As we have seen, Paula Hitler had said the same of Mimi—if only Adolf had married her the disasters of war might have been avoided, so she thought.

As far as his love-life was concerned, a repeated pattern emerges. Adolf falls for a teenager who then commits or attempts suicide when Adolf at first fascinates, then over-controls, and finally neglects her. Probably these suicidal events revived his feelings of guilt over his mother's death. He may have wondered how far he had brought this on by ignoring his mother's wishes that he work harder at school and find a proper job. She had had such high hopes for him and he had failed her. Now, as Führer, so he might have fantasised, he was making amends. Kreuger wrote: 'Hitler's failure to find a mate is at the core of his failure as a human being and is the source of his demonic, destructive spirit.' After Geli died in 1930, Adolf had sent Rudolf Hess to find his old flame Mimi and, for a while, they were reunited and, according to Mimi, had again enjoyed normal sexual relations. But Adolf had already met the attention-craving Eva Braun in 1929. She was then a rebellious seventeen year-old, just out of convent school, who had taken a job working as an assistant to Hitler's photographer, Heinrich Hoffmann. Hitler one day had seen her up a ladder reaching for a file and Eva had noticed this 'elderly gentleman' with 'a funny moustache' looking at her legs. She had liked it. Nobody knows when Adolf and Eva first became lovers but it was, according to Sayer and Botting, probably in early 1932, some five months after Geli's death, and shortly before Adolf was appointed Chancellor. Eva would joke that their fumblings had taken place on the same grand sofa upon which British premier Neville Chamberlain would later perch when trying to prevent the Second World War. It would still be another thirteen years before Eva and Adolf would be married, on the eve of their mutual suicides in the Berlin bunker in April 1945. What an extraordinary love-story! During the 1930s Adolf had flirted with other women, including some pretty actresses, but they came and they went. It appears that there were only three young women with whom Adolf ever had real sexual relationships—first it was Mimi in 1926 (when Adolf was thirty-seven), then Geli from 1926 until her death in 1930, then briefly Mimi again, and finally Eva. Eva's schoolmaster father had initially disapproved strongly about the relationship but Adolf had pulled rank and subdued him. That struggle at least was won.

Traudl Junge commented after the war that

> Eva Braun was a comfort to him ... in any case, he didn't have a very strong feeling for sex. Even with Eva Braun it was just a warm sort of feeling he had for her. She was one of the few people who had his absolute trust. Her fidelity was what was important to him. Not anything else. He adored her for that.

She would never let him down. (Even his mother had done that by submitting to his father and, then, by dying.) Above all, rather like his dogs, Eva 'worshipped' him devotedly. As with Mimi, she had been just an ordinary shop girl and twenty-three years his junior. So he felt at ease, fatherly and strong in her presence. She was his perfect woman—'a cute, cuddly, naïve little thing.' Furthermore, she was also just a little like a mother towards him. Adolf was only really at ease with those who reminded him of his fellow childhood victims on the receiving end of his father's violence—mother-figures, little sister-figures, and dogs! For Eva, Adolf was certainly the great love of her short life. But why? Junge explains: 'He was an exciting man to meet ... he had a radiance ... he was very charming.' Besides, Eva had endured her own struggle with her father and Adolf had won that battle for her; so they were comrades in arms as father-fighters and, crucially, he had rescued her from her father's control. He was shining knight and she was rescued damsel.

Adolf's core dynamic

Anti-semitism was already rife in the subcultures of Munich and Vienna where Adolf had been living and many blamed the disastrous defeat of 1918 upon politicians and Jews. As so often with Adolf he picked up ideas that were in the air and carried them to extremes. (This is true, for example, of his glorification of war—a positive attitude towards war had long been a feature of German culture.) By 1930 his anti-semitism was abnormally intense even for the society he lived in, and even more extreme than that of most of his Nazi followers. Why? Many theories have been put forward. First, one has to add a word of caution. Paranoid (persecutory) ideas and even delusions of this sort are quite common in bi-polar mood disorders (which Adolf appears to have suffered from mildly). They are symptoms that seem to come from nowhere, or rather, from inside the patient's head. External events may or may not be of importance in such cases. Historians, apparently unaware of this, have tended to look for simple *external* reasons for Hitler's anti-semitism, and some half a dozen such theoretical 'causes' have been proposed including:

(1) Adolf's experience of Dr Eduard Bloch, the Jewish doctor who had attended Adolf's mother when she died;

(2) the rejection of Adolf by the (Jewish?) examiners at the Academy of Arts in Vienna;

(3) allegedly catching syphilis from a Jewish prostitute;

(4) Adolf's perceived rejection by Stephanie Izak, who was not Jewish although Adolf may have been deceived by her surname into believing that she was;

(5) being swindled by his Jewish associates in pre-war Vienna;

(6) some undisclosed and guilt-creating sexual experience with a Jewish woman or man, perhaps around 1918/1919, or a combination of the above.

We shall never know for *certain* if any such external events were significant in the formation of Adolf's devastating anti-Jewish delusional system. But, for me, there is one outstanding probable cause—and that is *Adolf's belief, conscious or half-conscious, that his sadistic father was partly Jewish, and his fervent desire to protect the memory of his mother from this man*. If so, then Adolf was unwittingly following in the footsteps of Europe's previous greatest persecutor of Jews, Thomas Torquemada of the Spanish Inquisition, who also had a Jewish grandparent—seemingly adopting a denial of his own Jewishness through extreme anti-semitism.

What is the evidence to support this hypothesis? Well, we first have to accept that the unconscious mind operates on a network of loose associations that are not, strictly speaking, rational. In Adolf's case there was an association in his mind of a number of issues that, for the sane onlooker, appear to be unconnected. Furthermore, in the unconscious mind, dead figures can remain alive and active. We have already noted that Adolf heard the rumours of Alois' Jewish paternity that were rife in the 1920s, and we know that he had commissioned research into this possibility in 1930 that apparently tended to confirm this. In other words, Adolf had reasonable grounds to believe in his own part-Jewishness (even if we rule out Krueger's claims that Adolf knew that Sachs could be his father). We also know that Adolf would rave repeatedly about Jewish men raping and defiling Aryan women, and there is that well known piece in *Mein Kampf* which we have already examined, where Adolf speaks of a boy witnessing attacks by his father on his mother—things which would make even a grown-up shudder'. Once, when asked why he suspected the Jews of being responsible for so many ills in his Reich, Hitler merely said, instead of his usual ranting—'personal reasons'. Maybe as a little boy, he had indeed seen his ogre of a father hitting or sexually assaulting his mother. We know that his father could be violent, drunken and libidinous. Furthermore, Adolf was never able fully to express his hatred and fear of his father and so these feelings could have become spread onto Jews in general. This sort of displacement does happen. The strange phrase 'morally infected' in the famous quote from *Mein Kampf*, echoes the words in the passages where he is describing prostitution and the mysterious sexual dangers of Viennese life, and it does seem likely that sexuality became associated in Adolf's mind with his (perceived) Austrian/Jewish father. So I think it is at least probable, that when attacking Jews, Adolf was in fact unconsciously attacking his father. Certainly the Jews became the general scapegoats for all his ills, including his own failures. Just as his father had indirectly sabotaged Adolf's education, scorned his oratory and opposed his artistic career, so the Jews were responsible, in his eyes, for everything else that went wrong, including their own destruction and the war itself. But for Adolf the Jews were far more than mere scapegoats relieving him of any sense of guilt or failure. Remember that the insightful Kubizek tells us that 'the authority of his father still remained, even after his (Alois') death, the force in the struggle with which Adolf developed his own powers', and Adolf himself admits in *Mein Kampf* that his father had unwittingly 'sown the seed' for his (Adolf's) future career. So for Adolf, the war *was* just that, psychologically speaking—his unfinished battle or 'struggle' with his father that had been interrupted by his father's premature death. By what is known as the Zeigarnik effect, such 'unfinished business' tends to persist far more tenaciously than do conflicts that are concluded.

Much of Adolf's political career, as well as the day-to-day decisions it entailed, were based upon a sound grasp of realities and common sense. Increasingly, however, patterns and peculiarities emerge that have a deeper and pathological origin. The *intensity* of Adolf's hatreds may have been augmented by his sexual frustration and by his fears of impotence, but their *direction* was surely dictated by his all-consuming central fantasy. The ultimately unnecessary attacks upon France, Poland, Britain, Russia and other nations followed. How far were these attacks all expressions of 'the struggle' he confusedly, and largely unconsciously, believed he was waging to rescue his mother from his (Jewish) father? Adolf certainly accused Britain, Poland, France and Russia, dominated as they all were, in his opinion, by the Jews, of traits he remembered and hated in his father, accusing them of 'cruelty', 'lack of moral restraint' and 'the brutality of the violent egoist.' Later, he even depicted Churchill as the 'undisciplined swine who is drunk for eight hours of every twenty-four'. This, too, sounds very much like Alois, his father.

Adolf's series of land-grabs in Europe became progressively more irrational and riskier as the years went by. To start with Adolf had simply reclaimed territories taken from Germany after the loss of the First World War. Then came the Germanification of a willing Austria. These were decisions taken in summer months and made some sort of political sense. But Adolf could not stop. He then marched into Czechoslovakia and Poland thus rashly and prematurely forcing France and Britain to declare war. Adolf reacted to opposition from Poland and the west with childish tantrums. Increasingly, his decisions revealed the pressures of his internal personal 'spoiled child' psychopathology. On 20 April 1939 he had celebrated his fiftieth birthday and suddenly it seemed to him that time was short—'the problems must be solved by *me*, and I can wait no longer'. What exactly Adolf thought that 'the problems' were, is unstated. Almost certainly he did not understand that his insatiable need to continue fighting was being driven largely by his unconscious desire to defeat his father. In his mind the Jews were everywhere—in every country—and he had to overcome them before it was too late. It was now all or nothing.

Psychotherapists have found that people often unconsciously transfer onto others the attitudes, feelings and relationships that they have learned in relating to members of their family and others in their childhood. In Adolf's case (as in Princess Diana's and Horatio Nelson's) such 'transference' assumes epic proportions. Adolf repeats with Rudolf Hess and Albert Speer the sort of 'brotherly' relationship he first experienced with his sole friend Kubizek. One can speculate that he transferred onto the Jews the hatred he really felt for his father, while for Germany and her 'Aryan' culture, he expresses the love he had for his blue-eyed mother. By winning the war (against his father) he would gain the beautifully redesigned 'living space' (*lebensraum*) his mother had always needed, unconsciously getting her away from 'the smallness and overcrowding of the rooms' (as cited in the famous excerpt from *Mein Kampf*) where, so he believes, violence and rape occur. *Lebensraum*—the theory that Germans needed more territory in which to live—was the chief reason given by the Nazis to justify the Second World War. Hitler was obsessed with *lebensraum.* But it was, of course, utter nonsense. There was already plenty of room in Germany for the Germans. Whenever one is faced with such a patently absurd reason for something serious one must, as a psychologist, begin to wonder whether the real reason is pathological. *Lebensraum* was another of those notions that Adolf had picked up in the early 1920s. It had been around for years. Adolf subtly changed it, however, by tying it in with his anti-semitism. *Lebensraum* was now to be sought in the East, he said, and not the West. The Reich would expand into Russia, thus destroying Bolshevism, a system that was, according to Adolf, created and controlled by Jews. *If my speculation is correct, then Adolf was unconsciously seeking living space for Aryans (his mother) by ousting the Jews (his father).* In his childhood, the Hitlers had never had a fixed home, and Adolf had been fascinated with large living spaces and architectural designs for years. As Junge reports, he had a great liking for huge rooms, and whatever Adolf built or designed reflected this craving for spaciousness. Was this all an expression of his unconscious concern for his mother's proper accommodation and safety? Fairly typically for a political narcissist, the claustrophobic Adolf was identifying himself with his nation. (Louis XIV, de Gaulle and Henry VIII did likewise.) But, like Nelson, he also identified his nation with his mother; although Germans themselves called Germany the 'Fatherland', Adolf frequently refers to it as the 'Motherland'. How often such soubriquets emerge from the lips of demagogues!

Walter Langer also noticed Adolf's clear identification of Germany with his mother—'all the emotions he had once felt for his mother became transferred to Germany'. As if trying to bring his mother back from the dead Adolf would, in some of his speeches, shout 'Germany must live! Germany must live!' It was one of his most obsessive slogans.

Lebensraum was, he said, about 'the survival of the German people' (i.e., *his mother*). If the Bolsheviks were to win the war then—'the German woman would be fair game for these beasts'. In *Mein Kampf* various phrases support the dynamic of secret maternal love and separation, for example:

> 'An unnatural separation from the great common Motherland ... '
>
> 'I appeal to those who, severed from the Motherland ... '
>
> '(They) long for the hour that will allow them to return to the arms of the beloved mother ... '
>
> 'The longing grew stronger to go there (Germany) where, since my early youth, I had been drawn by secret wishes and secret love.'

Other phrases are compatible with his obsession with the abuse of his mother: 'It must be possible that the German nation can live its life ... without being constantly molested', and his fantasy of maternal submission to Jewish influences: 'The state ... crawled on its belly before Marxism.'

The word 'rape' is scattered through the pages of *Mein Kampf* as if recalling the infant Adolf's vision of his mother being ravaged by his drunken father. Langer suggests that Adolf also identified Austria (and the 'depraved' Vienna with its large Jewish population) with his father, who had proudly worn an Austrian uniform. Adolf had, after all, chosen to enlist in the German army, and not the Austrian, in 1914. Germany (i.e., *his mother*) was 'fighting for her existence' Adolf said. In the 1920s he had wanted to end any alliance with 'the debauched dynasty' of Austria (i.e., *his father*)—'the quicker the better for the German nation (i.e., *his mother*)'. All this seems to support the view that Adolf's career was being driven by his unresolved hatred of his father—'if a people (i.e., *Adolf and his mother*) is to become free it needs pride and willpower, defiance, hate, hate and once again, hate!' Adolf also praised the battle of Königgrätz, where Prussia (Germany) had once defeated Austria (i.e., *his father*) seeing it as the true foundation of the German Reich. The Reich emerged, Adolf said, from 'a conscious and sometimes unconscious struggle for hegemony, from which struggle Prussia ultimately issued victorious'. Again the word 'struggle'.

The final days

Our last eye-witness account of Adolf's behaviour, written by someone who knew him well, is by Traudl Junge, one of Adolf's personal secretaries during the final period of the war. Junge lived in the same buildings as Adolf for the last two and a half years of his life, regularly sharing her meals with him. Often she had very little secretarial work to do and her real function, along with that of the three other secretaries in his immediate headquarters, appears to have been to provide Adolf with young female company. (Other dangerous Utopian cult leaders—Charles Manson and Jim Jones, for example—similarly surrounded themselves with a circle of female admirers.) Junge describes an extraordinarily relaxed and homely lifestyle where she and her colleagues would, on a daily basis, sit with Adolf over lunch and around the fire in the evenings, listening to his endless non-political banter about the dogs and his early life, watching him doze off intermittently, and dutifully staying with him until he eventually retired to bed, often in the early hours of the morning. Was his reluctance to go to bed a fear of his recurrent nightmares or just a symptom of his elevated moods? We do not know.

When in residence, Eva Braun would join them and they would form a contented family group around their apparently kindly Führer. Junge denies that they had any contact with Adolf's political life or attended his regular twice-a-day military meetings with his generals. Her account makes one realise that there are two Adolfs—the amiable 'private man' and the hate-filled political fanatic and mass murderer; the former is the Adolf he reveals to women and the latter the version he shows to most men. Only in the Berlin bunker, in the last few days of Adolf's life, when his empire is collapsing around him, do the barriers between the two Adolfs begin to break down. When the women, including Eva, begin to see the hateful side of their friend and leader they start to puzzle about which is the real Adolf. On 29 April 1945, despite Eva's desperate pleadings, her brother-in-law and possible lover, SS man Hermann Fegelein, was shot for treachery on Adolf's specific orders. He had certainly been working for the disloyal Himmler, but treachery was never proved on his part. But this drunken womaniser had also been flirting openly with Eva for some months and she had found him intensely attractive. Is it too far-fetched to imagine that Adolf saw some similarity in behaviour between Fegelein and his lecherous father? Was killing Fegelein a final act of Oedipal patricide? His death certainly seemed to clear the way, psychologically speaking, for Adolf's wedding to Eva only an hour or two later. By this untypical action, the openly ordered execution of a previous friend, Adolf finally reveals to the women his ruthless side.

He had already lectured Junge on his Nietzschean and (misunderstood) evolutionary theories:

> In nature the law of the struggle for survival has reigned from the first. Everything incapable of life, everything weak is eliminated. Only mankind and above all the church have made it their aim to keep alive the weak, those unfit to live, and people of an inferior kind.

So there would be no compassion for traitors like Fegelein and Himmler (who had tried to sue for peace with the Allies) and no pity for the weak. The German people, like his generals, had let him down. They would have to suffer the consequences. Adolf crucially misidentified evolutionary 'fitness' with military strength. Ashamed of his own weakness, he had espoused a Spartan hardness. Yet in the last days Adolf also showed moments of genuine altruism, urging his staff to leave him and try to save their own lives: 'Anyone who wants to go can go now. Everyone is free to do so.' Many left but others—Junge among them—chose to stay: 'I suddenly feel very sorry for Hitler. A hopelessly disappointed man, toppled from the greatest heights, broken, lonely.'

Only after Adolf and Eva had killed themselves on 30 April 1945 did Traudl Junge escape. Junge had asked Adolf if Nazism would be revived. 'No,' he had replied, 'National Socialism is dead. Perhaps a similar idea will arise in a hundred years.' Helpfully, Adolf had told his loyal staff how to commit suicide painlessly: 'The best way is to shoot yourself in the mouth. Your skull is shattered and you don't notice anything.'

Rather contrary to the impression given by Kubizek, Junge portrays Adolf as humorous, but then she mainly saw the side of his character that he kept for women. Adolf liked a good story and would often tease his senior staff. He laughed with Junge when she complained about the elaborate forms she had to fill in for her marriage, said they were nonsense and that he would speak to Himmler about it. When Eva remarked upon his increasing stoop (probably due to his Parkinsonism) he quipped that it was because of the heavy keys in his trouser pockets, adding 'if I stoop I'll match you better!' (i.e., for height). He could even laugh when someone said, as their enemies closed in, that they would soon be able to travel between the Eastern and Western fronts by suburban railway. It is not hard to see why his secretaries stayed with him for years. He treated them like his family, with constant kindness and good humour.

Adolf did have a few male friends such as Hans Baur (his pilot), Sepp Dietrich (his leading bodyguard) and Heinrich Hoffmann (his photographer) — all cheerful and reliable extraverts. They certainly were not his rivals in any way and none were father-figures. With his generals, however, Adolf was never at ease. At the end Adolf had joked that his epitaph should read 'He was the victim of his generals'. Adolf was loyal to his old friends even when, like Hoffmann, they became alcoholic or otherwise an embarrassment. In return, he was touched by their loyalties and outraged by their later betrayals — as in the cases of Göring and Himmler. As things went wrong, he blamed his generals and then everyone else, but never himself, at least openly. Almost to the end he continued to fabricate military fantasies, intermittently believing that there were several phantom divisions coming to his rescue. Yet at other times he was entirely realistic insisting, against some of his staff's self-deluding optimism, that the war was indeed lost. In general, he had shown his anger to men and his softness to women, as he had with his parents years earlier. In the bunker he wanted his women near him at all times, especially at night. Was this to protect him from the demon of his father that tormented him in his nightmares? Adolf would appear the dictator to male strangers but the kindly uncle to his friends. Throughout his life Adolf was driven by intense but half-concealed, hatred. But hatred of what or whom exactly? The Jews? The Bolsheviks? The Slavs? What was the real target and origin of his hatred? Where did it all come from? Once, when fulminating against 'the uncivilised brutes' of Bolshevism, he had said—'one day the world will understand what this struggle was about!' But did Adolf, himself, ever really understand what his struggle was about? Could he ever admit, even to himself, that it was all about his unfinished struggle with his father?

Junge, like many who worked closely with Adolf, did not immediately become aware of his extraordinary sense of specialness. Adolf concealed this behind a form of modesty. He saw himself merely as 'the *servant* of Providence' or 'the *instrument* of Fate'. Thus, for example, during the war years, he deprived himself of the pleasure of watching movies with Eva and the secretaries because he felt this would be immoral self-indulgence while others were fighting and suffering. Superstitiously, perhaps, he did not want to upset Providence. So there was, as Kubizek had noted, a lack of obvious vanity about Adolf. Junge was, therefore, surprised one day when she asked him why he had not married Eva and he replied:

> I don't want children of my own. I think the offspring of men of genius usually have a very hard time of it. People expect them to be just like their famous progenitor, and won't forgive them for being only average. And in fact most of them are feeble-minded.

She was amazed he could so casually describe himself as a genius and, quite suddenly, realised that she was working for a charming egomaniac. But then his whole entourage also regarded him as a genius. By 1947, when Junge wrote these memoirs, she could admit that there had been the two aspects to her employer—'personally modest and kindly, but as a Führer, a harsh megalomaniac, he lived for his mission.' For years, however, she had not noticed, or wanted to notice, his dark side. To her, Adolf had been 'a kindly paternal figure, he gave me a feeling of security, solicitude for me, safety.' Adolf certainly liked to care for women—as he had done for his mother. This caring behaviour had made it hard for Junge to see the evil that was there.

Conclusions

It has sometimes surprised English people that the Germans took so seriously the rather absurd-looking and jumped-up person of Adolf Hitler. Snobbish women in pre-war England, untouched by his eloquence, dismissed him as 'a frightfully vulgar little man with a toothbrush moustache'. But for the demoralised Germans, after the humiliation of the Versailles Treaty in 1919, Adolf was saying all the right things—he would put them back to work and make Germany great again. It was his oratory that moved them. People began to smile and laugh once more. Adolf inspired the stolid and uneducated with his hypomanic babble. Hypomania (see Glossary) typically has this uplifting effect upon an audience—indeed, it is almost a diagnostic feature of the condition. When analysed, as it appears in cold print, as in *Mein Kampf*, what is said does not seem so impressive but, in the presence of the speaker with flashing eyes, as the ideas pour forth, listeners themselves become enthused. Pressure of talk and flight of ideas can, all too easily, be mistaken for intelligence. Besides, Adolf, when in the presence of men, was always an actor. Women could sometimes glimpse the other Adolf—the artistic, narcissistic, abused, angry, insecure and bereaved little boy, but with men he acted the role of the leader, the soldier, the man of vision—the ruthless architect of the greater Germany. He, himself, believed in these roles. As Kershaw puts it—'Hitler, the nonentity, the mediocrity, the failure, wanted to live like a Wagnerian hero.' If anyone ever did, Adolf exemplified the psychological theories of his celebrated Austrian contemporary, Alfred Adler, who had postulated (at the exact time of Adolf's failed youth) that feelings of inferiority were fundamental in provoking a striving for power. Hitler's Reich can be seen, in Adler's terms, as one huge 'masculine protest' or 'over compensation' for the weakness that the young Adolf had felt at the hands of his bullying father and, subsequently, as a drop-out in Vienna. His fantasies of greatness are a compensatory defence against the reality of his failure. Adolf's later fears of impotence would, in Adlerian terms, further intensify this lust for power. But then, as we have seen, Adolf was also a case for that other great Viennese contemporary, Sigmund Freud, who would have viewed Adolf's 'Oedipal' love for his mother and struggle with his father as the origins of all his neurotic problems.

Minor disorders of mood, such as Adolf's, are often reactions to stress. Probably the capacity for hypomanic reaction, which is far from universal, runs in families—it seems to be partly genetically determined. (Nelson had it, too.) Sustained elevations of mood themselves can produce paranoid thinking—ideas of persecution as well as messianic ideas. Adolf certainly showed both. The Jews were seen as the persecutors and he was the saviour of Germany marked out by Providence. Notice that he replaced the anthropomorphic and paternal 'God' with the more abstract 'Fate' or 'Providence' which are, as Hession has observed—'further evidence of his rejection of the father-figure.' After several unsuccessful attempts on his life Adolf became more than usually elated, excitedly proclaiming his survival as yet further evidence of Providential protection—'yet more proof that Fate has chosen me.' On another occasion he had remarked—'I go with the certainty of a sleepwalker along the path laid out for me by Providence.' As Langer points out Adolf had had experiences as a child, and later, in the First World War, when others died or were killed around him while he was spared, apparently, or so he concluded, by Providence. (Churchill and Nelson similarly felt divinely protected.) Hypomania is like being 'high' on amphetamines; feelings of euphoria and personal brilliance occur. Experiencing these, together with accelerated thoughts and exhilarating cognitive associations, the patient often concludes that he is indeed a genius. Such people become impatient with the slowness and 'stupidity' of those around them.

Paranoid ideas seem to follow naturally. Adolf's beliefs about the Jews appear to have developed quite gradually, beginning possibly as early as 1908 but only emerging publicly when he was in his early thirties, and becoming increasingly rigid and unmoveable as the years passed. There is no evidence that they were a symptom of paranoid schizophrenia, but simply of Adolf's unusual personality, his life circumstances and the occasionally elevated moods. Adolf had had an extraordinary and brutalising roller-coaster of an early life. In his first thirty years he had suffered beatings from his father, the death of his beloved mother, near-starvation in Vienna and then the terrors of trench warfare. Rather suddenly he had then found himself the most powerful and admired man in Germany. This transformation of fortunes alone would be enough to destabilise many.

Adolf achieved his political eminence chiefly through his extraordinary oratory. He narcissistically adored his own speaking skills, developing them partly because his father had opposed them. Such oratory had been the weapon of his childhood rebellion, with which he had defeated his father in arguments. For the young Adolf rhetoric became the equivalent of music for a later generation of adolescent pop singers – it was a skill that made him the centre of mass attention and adulation.

After Adolf was made Chancellor in 1933 the usual hubris of political leaders amplified his dogmatism and he increasingly ignored the advice of dissenters. Like most of his cronies when they were tried at Nuremberg in 1946 he had never actually seen the cruel consequences of his policies. Like them, if he had been shown the Allied newsreels of the camps, he might have been unsettled. That is possibly why his 'office manager' in later years, Martin Bormann, ordered that no-one should raise such issues with him. Most of the other leading Nazis were ambitious, vain, ruthless and arrogant, but they were not especially cruel men. Nearly all had, like Adolf, experienced early failure, handicap and mediocrity. They had all felt inferiority feelings. They were mostly ill-educated, too, as Adolf was, and without the instilled psychological 'checks and balances' of members of a traditional ruling class. Isolated in their own newly gained worlds of comfort and importance, few had any real idea of the horrors of Auschwitz or the Eastern Front for which they were responsible. Except for most of Adolf's battlefield decisions, his vague and grandiose orders were filtered through half-a-dozen levels of Nazi bureaucracy before being put into effect by brutalised and brainwashed front line SS and Wehrmacht troops. These men merely 'obeyed orders' — as some sixty per cent of ordinary human beings of most cultures will do, even in peacetime, as the important research of Stanley Milgram has demonstrated. Meanwhile, Adolf remained cocooned in his fantasy world and, after 1943, isolated from real contact with the horrors of his Reich. Most of Hitler's staff in the last few months were also out of touch. As Junge writes: 'Hitler lived, worked, played with his dog, ranted and raged at his generals, ate meals with his secretaries, and drove Europe towards its fate — and we hardly noticed.' By the 1940s, the lethal distance between ruler and reality was increasing. Adolf was entirely obsessed with himself and, particularly, with his plans and ideas.

Adolf certainly compartmentalised his behaviour. As we have seen, there was one Adolf for women and another Adolf for men. The only row with a woman of which I have heard was the one with his lover Geli — and that had fatal consequences. Not only did Adolf make sharp distinctions between the way he behaved in the presence of men and women, and between his treatment of strangers and friends, but there was also a world of difference between his external social life and his inner world of fantasy. It was the latter that was always the most real to him. The world of ordinary social intercourse, of daily life, was a mere charade of secondary importance. As an actor he could go through the motions and act the part of an ordinary politician or an avuncular friend. But he always knew that his 'true' self, the genius Adolf, was entirely separate and, to him, more real. Always behind the soft feminine side he showed to women (his mother in him) and the harsh side he showed to men (his father in him) stood the messianic genius. Yet somehow, all these Adolfs were both real and acted. He was an actor whose medium of power was always his rhetoric. He was brilliantly eloquent but not deeply intelligent.

Although his paranoid fantasies about the Jews drove the dark side of the whole Reich, when Adolf discovered that one of his key personal staff, his cook Marlene von Exner, was part-Jewish, there was no crisis. He decided that, in order for him to set a good example, she had to leave, but he did not denounce her nor order her immediate internment. On the contrary, he furiously yelled at the unsympathetic Bormann that he wanted Marlene and her family to be fully protected. Needless to say they were. According to Junge, who was Marlene's friend, Adolf apologised to Marlene, arranged for her family to be 'Aryanised', invited her as his special guest to the Berghof and, after she left his employment, paid her a further six months' wages. In a sense, his deadly anti-semitism was purely 'theoretical'; there was nothing 'personal' about it. Was he using massive denial to conceal from himself the reality of the Holocaust or was he deliberately concealing his wickedness from the young ladies in his entourage? Junge relates how one of his women guests, Henriette von Schirach, one evening complained to Adolf that she had seen some Jews being badly treated in Amsterdam and asked whether he knew about it. 'There was a painful silence. Soon afterwards Hitler rose to his feet, said goodnight and withdrew.' To me, this appears to be the reaction of an entirely guilty man.

One of Adolf's main racial obsessions was his opposition to the mixing of the Jewish and Aryan races which would lead, so he thought, to 'weakness'. In his opinion, 'the lost purity of the blood alone destroys inner happiness for ever.' But, if my central hypothesis is correct, then Adolf consciously or unconsciously saw *himself* as the product of such a mixed union, and so must have feared that he was himself already a weak and polluted specimen. This could have been a further powerful source of his profound lack of self-esteem and also, for his anger towards his father.

At a deeply unconscious level he was irrationally angry with his mother, too, not just for abandoning him (by dying) but for marrying a partly Jewish man. We have already seen that he may also have fantasised that his parents married not for love but out of expediency. This also, so he believed, was a common cause of 'weakness' in offspring. Thus, Adolf probably blamed both his parents for the undoubted weakness he had felt as a skinny and 'impotent' little drop-out in his teens and twenties, and against which he compensated by seeking such devastating political power.

Diagnosis and treatment

Perhaps, in the modern world, Adolf might seek psychological treatment, at least for his occasional slight depressions and his fears of impotence. If so, what would a psychiatrist make of him? I think a competent professional would give him the diagnostic label of Narcissistic Personality Disorder (NPD) with mild Bipolar Disorder (Cyclothymia). This, at least, is the modern American psychiatric terminology that I believe best fits Adolf. NPD is a condition found more often in men than women and is believed to affect around 1 per cent of the general population. Hales' and Yudofsky's description of Narcissistic Personality Disorder is as follows:

> A pervasive pattern of grandiosity (in fantasy or behaviour), need for admiration, and lack of empathy, beginning by early adulthood and present in a variety of contexts, as indicated by five (or more) of the following:
>
> (1) has a grandiose sense of self-importance (e.g. exaggerates achievements and talents, expects to be recognized as superior without commensurate achievements);

(2) is preoccupied with fantasies of unlimited success, power, brilliance, beauty, or ideal love;

(3) believes that he or she is 'special' and unique and can only be understood by, or should associate with, other special or high-status people (or institutions);

(4) requires excessive admiration;

(5) has a sense of entitlement, i.e. unreasonable expectations of especially favourable treatment or automatic compliance with his or her expectations;

(6) is interpersonally exploitative, i.e. takes advantage of others to achieve his or her own ends;

(7) lacks empathy: is unwilling to recognize or identify with the feelings and needs of others;

8) is often envious of others or believes that others are envious of him or her;

(9) shows arrogant, haughty behaviours or attitudes.

Adolf certainly exhibited items 1, 2, 3 and 5 in the above definition but, to qualify technically, he requires an additional item. This is more questionable. Adolf did not excessively demand admiration, or lack empathy with those he knew personally, or appear envious of others, nor was he particularly haughty. However, he utterly lacked empathy (item 7) with all his many real or imagined adversaries, and especially with those he never, or rarely, met. For him, such groups as 'Slavs' and 'Jews' did not exist as real people; they had become mere ideas in his head. I suppose we could also characterise Adolf as arrogant, but that is borderline. More probably we could accurately accuse Adolf of item (6)—he was 'interpersonally exploitative', at least as far as his enemies were concerned. To his friends he could be remarkably loyal, but to huge numbers of those with whom he was personally unacquainted, especially to groups of persons in the abstract, (e.g., gypsies, the mentally handicapped, non-Austro-Germans generally, Bolsheviks, Slavs and, of course, Jews), he was indeed ruthlessly exploitative and destructive. Adolf showed a clear and narcissistic tendency to treat those whom he had met quite differently from those he had not. Once someone had had tea with Adolf, his visitor's life was a great deal safer than it would be have been had he had a drink with Stalin. Adolf did not usually destroy his 'friends'—whereas Stalin certainly did. Adolf's justification for his ruthless exploitation of others was, of course, not on the basis of material gain but because of the 'specialness' of his goals, which is another peculiarly narcissistic feature. What was strange and rather unusual about Adolf was that his narcissism was tempered by a sort of personal mildness; the kindly Adolf he showed to women. He was a sensitive and obsessional kind of narcissist. Yet there were few compromises in Adolf's fantasy world; almost everything was one way or the other. On one side were the forces of good with himself at their head: mother, Germany, Aryans, Wagner, women, grand architecture and nature. On the other side were father, Jews, foreigners, Marxism, men and racial impurity.

Could there have been some even deeper currents at work in Adolf's psyche? Was he really a far more disturbed person, driven by huge and partially repressed sadistic impulses, denying fiercely his latent homosexuality of which he was ashamed, recklessly and deliberately destroying his Reich and himself, concealing the delusions and hallucinations of a paranoid schizophrenic? There are those who believe that he was some of these things, but there is a lack of evidence.

A good diagnostician would, of course, certainly recognise that Adolf also suffered from a number of subordinate problems, most obviously his sexual difficulties and his mild Cyclothymia or bipolar mood swings (as narcissists quite often show). Today, all these could be helped with treatment, although the underlying personality disorder itself would probably remain entrenched. Cyclothymia is defined as the presence (for two years or more) of numerous episodes with hypomanic symptoms and frequent depressive periods (that do not fit the criteria for *major* depression or mania), that are unaccountable by other disorders, and cause social, occupational or other impairments. Patients usually respond well to treatment with Lithium.

Adolf was not an original philosopher. He was, however, an effective propagandist for ideas that had been in circulation for decades — the romantic nationalism, expansionism and anti-semitism of the old *völkisch* movement. Nazism was just a new name for all this. It was Adolf's emotive oratory that persuaded the masses to support these ideas, and the success of his oratory was in large part due to the fanatical sincerity of his own commitment. This sincerity turned him into a religious leader for millions of Germans who were seeking certainty. Where did his fanaticism originate? It came from Adolf's personal psychopathology. Unconsciously he had injected his own psychodynamics—his narcissism, his love of his mother and hatred of his father—into the existing framework of the *Völkisch* (Nazi) ideology. Narcissists can do this; they project themselves onto the world and see links between themselves and big external events. For Adolf, *völkisch* ideas happened to fit around his personal emotions like a gauntlet. It was his own private frustrations and hatreds, shoe-horned into this iron fist, that powered the whole Reich. *His struggle with his father drove not only his anti-semitism but became the Second World War itself.*

The danger is that something like this could so easily happen again. Out-of-touch leaders, in love with their own ideas, may have little vivid understanding of what their orders mean in terms of the all-too-real sufferings of those affected by them. Armed with spin doctors they may launch a nation intemperately into war on spurious or imagined grounds, that may (or may not) have some hidden origin in their personal psychodynamics. The narcissist, enflamed by messianic, religious or persecutory fantasies, gives the commands, and the obedient rank and file obey. (Normal people can do terrible things if they find themselves parts of a terrible system.) So we need to beware of ordinary-looking, plausible and well-mannered men or women who become prime ministers or presidents—and especially if they are narcissistic fantasists with a modicum of eloquence and charisma.

Sources

Bullock, Alan, *Hitler and Stalin : Parallel Lives* (London: Harper Collins, 1991)

Bullock, Alan, *A Study in Tyranny*, revised edn (Harmondsworth: Penguin, 1962)

Eberle, Henrik and Uhl, Matthias eds, *The Hitler Book:The Secret Dossier Prepared for Stalin* (London: John Murray, 2005)

Fitzgerald, Michael, *Adolf Hitler: A Portrait* (Spellmount, 2006)

Golumb, Elan, *Trapped in the Mirror : Adult Children of Narcissists in their Struggle for Self* (New York: William Morrow, 1992)

Hales, Robert E. and Yudofsky, Stuart C., *Essentials of Clinical Psychiatry*, 2nd edn (Washington & London: American Psychiatric Publishing Inc., 2004)

Hanfstaengl, Ernst, *Hitler: The Missing Years* (London, 1957)

Hanisch, Rheinhold, *I Was Hitler's Buddy* (New Republic, April 1939)

Hession, Michael, *Personal Communication*, October 2007

Hitler, Adolf, *Mein Kampf* (1924), tr. Ralph Manheim (London: Pimlico, 1992)

Junge, Traudl, *Until the Final Hour – Hitler's Last Secretary* ed. Melissa Müller (Munich: Ullstein Heyne, 2002), English tr. Anthea Bell (London: Weidenfeld & Nicolson, 2003)

Kershaw, Ian, *Hitler 1889–1936: Hubris* (Harmondsworth: Penguin, 1998)

Kershaw, Ian, *Hitler 1936–1945: Hubris* (Harmondsworth: Penguin, 2000)

Krueger, Kurt, *I was Hitler's Doctor: His Intimate Life* (New York: Avalon, 1941, republished by Biltmore, 1943)

Kubizek, August, *The Young Hitler I knew*, intro. Ian Kershaw (London: Greenhill, 2006; first published in Germany in 1953).

Langer, Walter, *The Mind of Adolf Hitler* (Basic Books, 1943: New York, 1972)

Lewis, David, *The Man who Invented Hitler* (Headline, 2003)

Lloyd, Rachel, *Personal Communication*, 1960

Milgram, Stanley, *Obedience to Authority: An Experimental View* (London: Harper Collins, 1974)

Owen, David, *In Sickness and in Power* (London: Methuen, 2008)

Oxlade, Robert:,*Personnel Communication*, October, 2007

Reiter, Mimi, 'I was Hitler's lover', *Sunday Pictorial*, May–June, 1959

Sayer, Ian and Botting, Douglas, *Hitler and Women: The Love Life of Adolf Hitler* (London: Robinson, 2004)

Speer, Albert, *Spandau: The Secret Diaries* (London: Collins, 1976)

Diana Spencer, Princess of Wales

Chapter 3
Diana Spencer

1961–1997

The magical food of love

Lady Diana Spencer married Prince Charles on 29 July 1981 when she was aged just twenty. Within months, due to her good works, curious behaviour and radiant beauty, she had become one of the most celebrated women in the world. In August 1996 Diana and Charles were divorced. A year later Diana died in a car crash in Paris.

I remember meeting Diana shortly after she was married. How could I ever forget? She was literally radiant. She glowed. Her cheeks were flushed and her eyes shone. Her small talk, too, sparkled. She was, I reflected at the time, a beautiful young woman who was desperate to be the centre of attention and approval, and there must be some devastating reason for this. The Princess made an indelible impression on me.

Diana Spencer was born into an upper class home in Norfolk. She might have gone on to lead an ordinary life typical of hundreds of other women of her background, bringing up a family of her own and mingling with the 'county' set. She was not intellectually brilliant, nor ambitious for wealth or power. So how did she become an international star—an icon whose memory will remain with us for decades? One answer is that she married the heir to the British throne. So was this royal marriage purely a matter of chance or did she, or her relations, somehow cause it to happen? And was it the only reason for her celebrity?

Like all my subjects in this book, Diana's life has been thoroughly scrutinized by historians and is the subject of a number of impressive biographies. Whereas there is general agreement among writers that Nelson was a heroic genius and that Hitler was an utter villain, there is no such consensus about Diana. Instead, there are two quite distinct camps that see her either as a manipulative trouble maker or as a near-saint who was mistreated by the royal family and by most of the media. This present study avoids either extreme, but concludes that Diana was a deeply disturbed and unhappy person.

The family

The Spencers are old English Whig aristocracy. Like many such families their mannered exteriors during the 1960s and 1970s hid the usual amount of emotional difficulties to which human beings are heirs, nobility providing no defence against psychological dysfunction. In Diana's family there were, for example, quite obvious personality problems in two of her grandparents: her father's father ('Jack', the 7th Earl Spencer) and her mother's mother (Ruth, Lady Fermoy). In their turn, no doubt, some of Jack and Ruth's disturbing traits could be attributed to the influence of their own forebears. Such disturbances can run down the generations, and are not necessarily genetically determined, but culturally.

Jack (like many Spencers, his real name was John) was known as the 'Curator Earl' on account of his obsessive concern for the family seat, Althorp, and its contents. He has variously been described as 'irascible, difficult and eccentric', 'a crashing snob' who 'disliked any human contact, particularly with the lower orders', and was 'abrupt to the point of rudeness', having 'no time whatever for fools', being 'relentlessly taciturn' and 'not seeing the point of ordinary people'. One biographer has gone further in calling Jack 'a monster' who was 'mean and nasty and cruel'. His grandson Charles (the 9th Earl), an astute observer, has written that 'he induced respect in many and fear in almost all'. Other relatives found him 'very frightening when we were small'. Jack Spencer died in 1975 when Diana was nearly fourteen. She had hardly known him, but he must have provided, on her occasional and disliked childhood visits to Althorp, a model of masculine fierceness. To be fair to Jack, such behaviour was not uncommon at the time. Upper class men were expected to be bluff, autocratic and curmudgeonly. Underneath, as Charles Spencer has suggested, may have lain hurt, depression, and a sense of childhood rejection. The cantankerous exterior was a defence, but it was a defence that would affect Diana through the impact it had upon her own father Johnnie (the future 8th Earl Spencer). Jack and Johnnie did not get along at all easily. As a boy, Johnnie would dread the train journey home from school and would hide in the corner of the carriage hoping his father would forget to meet him at the station and, when at Althorp, would sometimes hide from his father's wrath by climbing into the space above the bathroom ceiling. Jack regarded his son as unintelligent, and Johnnie made the mistake of showing little interest in his father's passions—the history of the family and the house. He preferred parties and sports and was close to his beautiful and sensitive mother, Cynthia Hamilton, who has been described by Charles Spencer as 'saintly' and 'a paragon of sweet nobility'. Cynthia died in 1972 when Diana was aged only eleven but she had made an impression upon the child. Not only did her looks resemble those of Diana but Diana also seems, in adulthood, to have emulated her kindly grandmother's concern for the sick and suffering, half-believing that Cynthia was watching over her from heaven.

The other obviously dysfunctional family member was of far greater consequence for Diana's development: her mother's mother, Ruth Fermoy. Ruth came from an ambitious middle class Scottish background whose males had made money as paint-manufacturers. As a girl of twenty,

Ruth, a talented pianist and a beautiful young woman, had been sent to study at the Conservatoire of Music in Paris where in 1931 she had met and married the rich Maurice Roche, 4th Baron Fermoy. The portly Maurice was over twenty years her senior and had been brought up in New York by his American mother. The ambitious Ruth had been courting Maurice's younger twin brother Frank, but had quickly changed allegiance when she met the brother with the Irish title. It may be difficult for some modern readers to understand that in mid-twentieth century Britain an obsession with social class was almost universal, particularly among the middle classes, and social climbing was often the dominant motive in life. Class frequently mattered more than parental love, fame, politics or religion. It could even, on occasion, matter more than money itself. Before the days of the twenty-first century's cult of celebrity, social class was, for many, considered to be not only the index of a person's worth and importance, but virtually the be-all and end-all of existence. So it was for Ruth Fermoy. Recent biographers have described her as 'having a Scottish steel about her' and being 'a manipulative, self-absorbed snob'. The Fermoys had been, in some respects, outsiders in the upper echelons of pre-war English society, not only trying to live down their undoubted Irish, American and partly middle class origins, but also, according to one writer, anxiously concealing any reference to one of Ruth's great great grandmothers, Eliza, who had been both unmarried and a native of Bombay. Maurice Fermoy had settled in Norfolk in the late 1920s and been elected the Conservative MP for Kings Lynn. Initially the family had been cold-shouldered by the local gentry, but had then been taken up by the nearby royals, Maurice becoming a regular shooting guest at the Royal family's residence at Sandringham, and Ruth eventually being made the Queen Mother's Woman of the Bedchamber. During the 1930s the Fermoys took the lease on the royals' guest accommodation, Park House, on the Sandringham Estate. Ruth, it has been said, 'showed a flinty desire to rise in the world' and once she had done so, she stayed there, carefully guarding her position at Court above all other considerations, until her death in 1993. Ruth's importance for Diana's psychological growth was not only as a model of machination and manipulation, but also in providing her with a mother whose behaviour would prove crucial in the development of Diana's own disordered personality.

Diana's mother

The Fermoys (Ruth and Maurice) had three children, all of whom, unsurprisingly in view of Ruth's cold unsuitability for motherhood, were to lead unhappy lives. Her son Edmund (born in 1939) duly became the 5th Baron Fermoy and, after a history of depression, shot himself in 1984. Ruth Fermoy was determined to marry off her two daughters to the most eligible titled husbands she could find for them, and she did well; her eldest daughter Mary (born in 1934) marrying Anthony Berry, the son of Viscount Kemsley, and Frances (born in 1936 and destined to be Diana's mother) in 1954 marrying 'Johnnie' Spencer, then Viscount Althorp and the heir to the Spencer Earldom and to the Althorp estates.

Frances was, in many ways, the typical product of rich and aspiring parents of the post-war era. She adored her warm, ebullient and flirtatious father, Maurice, describing him as 'the most compassionate, sensitive and glorious man I have ever met.' Like many women who idealise their fathers, she would later find her husbands disappointing. The first, Johnnie Spencer, was, however, very much to her mother's liking. The Spencers could, after all, trace their family back to the mid-fifteenth century and had been Earls for two hundred years. By marrying her daughter into the Spencer lineage Ruth would be further securing her own social position. The Spencers were not only aristocratic they were, unlike the Fermoys and even the royals themselves, indubitably English. In 1952 Ruth discovered, much to her alarm, that Johnnie had become unofficially engaged to Lady Anne Coke, the nineteen year-old daughter of her neighbour the Earl of Leicester.

Undeterred, Ruth entertained Anne at her house in London and encouraged her to invite her young man around for drinks. When Johnnie Spencer arrived he was subjected to Ruth's expert charm and, on his next visit, introduced to her fifteen year old daughter Frances who was 'unexpectedly' home from boarding school. Tina Brown describes the process convincingly:

> *WHOOMPH!* That was the word Frances used to Hannah Gilmour when she described the immediate attraction she felt for Johnnie Spencer. Gilmour remembers it clearly because Frances used it again fifteen years later when Frances fell madly in love with the heir to a wallpaper fortune Peter Shand Kydd. At fifteen Frances was in that appealing transition age between schoolgirl and socialite, but her height made her seem much older. 'And suddenly,' Anne (Coke) recalled, 'I could see that Lady Fermoy was pushing Frances like mad. 'Do you like tennis, Johnnie? Oh, Frances adores tennis, don't you, Frances? Do you like swimming? Oh, Frances just *adores* swimming, don't you Frances?' and Frances just stood there and simpered. Afterwards Johnnie said to me, 'What a simply marvellous girl Frances is!' and I thought no more about it. But the next time I saw him he said, 'The most beautiful pair of stockings arrived for me knitted by Frances at school!' You can guess whose idea that was! Soon Anne started to perceive coolness in her fiancé. 'I was devastated when Johnnie dropped me,' she admitted. 'I was sent off on the QE to America ostensibly to sell Holkham pottery, but really to get over it.'

If ever there was an arranged marriage then this was it. Blinded by her school girl passion it would not be for some years that Frances would begin to notice that she and her husband had little in common. While he was intellectually dull, she was bright and high-spirited. The seeds of disaster had been sown. Besides, as Frances matured she began to question her mother's priorities. Surely there was more to life than mere snobbery and social climbing? Obediently, however, she did what she had to do by breeding Spencer children, hoping for a son and heir. Two daughters, Sarah and Jane, were born in 1955 and 1957, and then, at last, the longed-for son John in 1960. Tragically, the baby boy was severely deformed and died within a few hours. Probably for the kindest of motives Johnnie decreed that his wife should not see this child, although this action would later be construed by some biographers as an act of cruelty. (There was an upper class doctrine, probably engendered by the terrors of two world wars, that held that it was best not to see some horrors so as to avoid being haunted by them.) For Diana, this baby's death would duly assume almost mythic importance and was used by her as a pain-reducing, but only partially complete, explanation for what was to befall her. Although clearly fertile, Frances was obliged to undergo medical tests to ascertain her ability to bear a son, and again became pregnant. On 1 July 1961, at Park House, she gave birth to another girl who was, after a delay of a few days, named Diana.

It would be helpful if we could know more exactly the real feelings of Diana's parents at this moment in their lives. Regrettably, all this remains unclear. If they did feel disappointment or a lack of love towards the new baby they quickly took trouble to conceal such feelings. As far as observers were concerned, little Diana was rapidly accepted and, indeed, appeared to become her father's favourite. Not for three years did Frances fall pregnant again but eventually, in May 1964, she at last produced a boy, Charles.

On the whole, servants from that era have spoken well of Frances—'She treated me and the others like friends rather than staff' one recalls 'and she spent a lot of time in the nursery ... she would always be there in the evening for cuddles and bedtime stories.' The reference to 'cuddles' is important.

Biographers are not agreed as to when, exactly, Johnny and Frances' marriage began to break down. Maybe it had never really existed. Frances herself may not have had a clear example from her own mother (Ruth) as to what a healthily relaxed marriage could be all about. Her mother was certainly strong, determined and ambitious but she was more of a dutiful than a doting wife. Ruth had put her daughter through the sort of upper class education that was normal for the period, and this had given Frances a set of good manners and limited expectations, but not much by way of useful professional skills or an understanding of human nature. She was, however, a bouncy schoolgirl and, as we have seen, had been bowled over at the age of fifteen when introduced to the handsome Johnnie Spencer, with whom her mother had carefully encouraged her to form a relationship. Sex, having children and finding herself to be Lady Althorp, were all exhilarating and demanding occupations for the first few years of marriage but then the excitement began to wear off. While Frances was continuing her development, her husband's had stopped or even gone into reverse. He was no longer the dashing young guardsman but had become a staid middle-aged gentleman-farmer with boring friends. Johnnie, like any weak man with an ancient title, a great house and a lot of land, easily attracted social climbers and hangers-on. There was no need for him to be interesting. Like a beautiful woman he could, without too much effort, remain the centre of attention, despite his dullness. But Johnnie was becoming increasingly dull just at the time when the intelligent Frances, who had been a mother for ten years, was beginning to seek a wider range of interests. By the time she was a bored thirty-year-old, who had been engaged at seventeen and married at eighteen, she was desperate for adventure. Unlike some wives who find themselves in this position, and who just settle for a life of muddling through and making do with local charities and flower-shows, Frances was, all too like her mother, a woman of determination and apparent confidence. So she *did* something about her boredom. She started to go to London to seek new intellectual and, as it inevitably turned out, amorous excitements. She is described at this time as being 'very attractive and blonde and sexy with such joie de vivre and fun about her'. She was wealthy, too, and indeed it was her money and not her husband's that had financed their married life in Park House, which had been leased to them by Ruth Fermoy from 1955. (Was Ruth already, at this early stage, plotting a royal marriage for her grandchildren by ensconcing them upon the royal estate?)

DIANA'S CHILDHOOD FAMILY

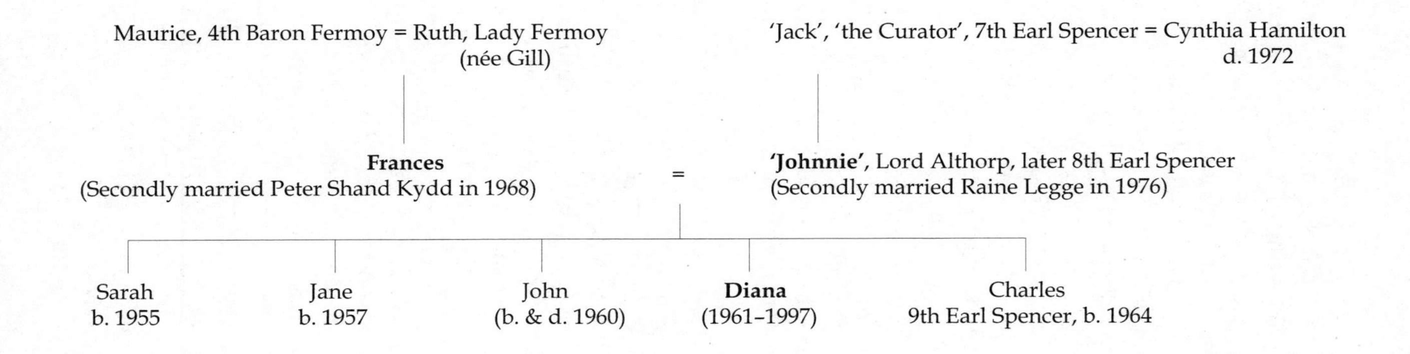

Some biographers date the onset of Frances' marriage breakdown to the moment that she met and fell in love with Peter Shand Kydd in the swinging London of 1966, while others see it as a 'post-natal' reaction after she gave birth to Charles in 1964. A third group date it even earlier, to the birth of Diana in 1961 or to the death of baby John in 1960. Yet, surely this arranged marriage was, emotionally-speaking, doomed from its contrived beginnings in 1954. Today, a dynamic young woman like Frances would follow her own career. How could someone like her, bursting with drive and ability, be expected to endure for ever the increasing boredoms and isolation of living in the Norfolk countryside? It is rather surprising, at least by modern standards of endurance, that the marriage lasted as long as it did. Yet, when the inevitable happened, with a trial separation in 1967, everyone in the stuffy upper class circles in which she moved, blamed Frances. In particular, and predictably, her coldly furious mother Ruth blamed her, too. Ruth, unable to accept that her daughter was anything much more than a cipher in her dynastic stratagems, and infuriated by Frances' romance with a man from a very similarly modest background to her own, put the blame for the divorce firmly upon her daughter. In order to avoid any blame for the failed marriage being attributed to herself, Ruth even took to blaming her late husband's American genes. The lady did, indeed, protest too much.

After her second divorce in 1988, Frances would take up religion and good works, living an increasingly lonely and unhappy life in Scotland, and dying in 2004. Shortly before her death, in a series of meetings with Mike Merritt, Frances outlined her considerable antipathy towards the 'cold and selfish' Royal Family, describing her own mother's 'close friend' the Queen Mother as 'quite a bitch'. She attributed Diana's frequent bouts of hostility towards her as due to her maternal attempts at control: 'As you can imagine in her (Diana's) life there were not too many people who said 'No' ... so therefore, when I did, it wasn't anything but doubly unpopular.' In these interviews Frances sounded angry, outspoken and lacking in refined judgement. Some of this may have been caused by her illness at the time, but it seems, hardly surprisingly, that Frances had been a disturbed person for most of her life. For years she had experienced feelings of misery which she bravely tried to conceal under loud laughter, jolly extraversion or lofty brusqueness. After the loss of baby John, so she recalled: 'One had to keep a stiff upper lip and get on with it.' Her mother had told her that 'worse things happen at sea!' As a nanny later said: 'Lady Althorp was a wonderful woman—always laughing. Diana, rather proudly, would follow this example. 'I'm like Mummy,' she said, years later. 'I can be utterly miserable inside, but outside I'm happy and smiling and no-one will ever have a clue as to how I feel.' Significantly, Frances would describe both her own marriage, and her daughter's, as 'mirages of happiness'. To an extent, Frances had married Johnnie simply to please her mother Ruth, for whom appearances were almost all that mattered.

Diana's father

Diana's father, Johnnie Spencer, must have had a difficult childhood in view of his own father's strange and intimidating personality. As his son Charles has pointed out, Johnnie 'felt the *froideur* of a parent not fully engaged emotionally in their relationship.' I have already reported little Johnnie's fear of his father and that he sometimes hid from him in the false ceiling above the bathroom. He was, however, close to his saintly mother Cynthia, and he grew up into a man who was 'tall, strapping and handsome, with a powerful sex drive.' Once out of Eton he had joined the Army. In the war, as a young subaltern in the Scots Greys, Johnnie saw action, did well, and was mentioned in despatches. After the war he had become ADC to the Governor of South Australia and then an equerry to the Queen. When Frances had first met him he had appeared worldly and interesting, but gradually the scales fell from her eyes.

A friend has remarked that Johnnie had 'always been duller than ditchwater, but she didn't notice at first ... He didn't ever want to come up to town. To go to the theatre.

Ruth Fermoy
Diana's ambitious maternal grandmother.

Frances Shand Kydd
Diana's mother, who left her when she was six.

To see concerts.' His commanding officer had described him as 'very nice but very stupid' and even his former fiancée, Lady Anne Coke, said 'Johnnie was the best of company when he was a young man, but then he just became boring, wrapped up in his children and his country life.' In general he was described as endearingly down to earth, 'charming and impeccably bred'. Yet there may have been some contradictory qualities, as a few found him 'unkind' or 'odd and unpredictable and moody'. Like a true aristocrat he had the common touch and, as a reaction against his father's curmudgeonly aloofness, told his children to 'treat everybody as an individual and never throw your weight around.' He tried to be a good a parent but was sometimes absent, either physically or emotionally, leaving his children to the care of others. As Andrew Morton puts it:

> (He) sometimes joined the children for tea in the nursery but, as their former nanny Mary Clarke recalled, 'it was very hard going. In those early days he wasn't very relaxed with them.' Johnnie buried himself in his work for Northamptonshire County Council, the National Association of the Boys' Clubs and his cattle farm. Charles recalled: 'He was really miserable after the divorce, basically shell-shocked. He used to sit in his study the whole time. I remember occasionally, very occasionally, he used to play cricket with me on the lawn. That was a great treat.'

Johnnie was not of the generation that touched or cuddled or felt entirely at ease with children. After the divorce he was obviously depressed. One biographer asserts that he used to hit his wife Frances, but the others do not endorse this, nor did she. Most see him as being weakly subordinate to her strong will. He had thought his marriage was a happy one and was shattered when Frances had left.

Charles Spencer's loyal and affecting comments about his parents are even-handed and rather optimistic: 'We had very loving parents, who cared for us in their separate homes with devotion, humour, honesty and respect', he says. 'I feel lucky to have had two parents who did so much for us; both had immense qualities.' Both parents, in their own ways, did, indeed, love their children, but, all too often, for hours or even days at a time, one or both of them were not there and the children were, at least emotionally, alone and deprived.

Diana's siblings

Diana's oldest sibling is Sarah who was six years older than her, and has been described as 'complex' and 'very strong, very alive and alert'. As a child she appeared confident and intelligent. Diana hero-worshipped her. Jane, her next sister, has been seen as a far less assertive child. She was 'always the sensible one, responsible, quiet and bookish with brown-haired, unremarkable looks'. Diana was born eighteen months after little John's demise. He had died when only a few hours old but his death, and the disappointment this had caused her parents, continued to be felt. His grave, in a local churchyard, was visited by members of the family. Diana, as a young child, was aware of this recent family tragedy and must have drawn her own infantile conclusions. Charles, born when Diana was three, was unhappy as a toddler, describing himself as 'an introspective and shy little boy'. After the separation, Diana recalled his sobbing alone at night, felt close to him and believed they had much in common—'Like me he will always suffer.' Charles, however, unlike Diana, did well at school work.

Diana

Diana once claimed that 'being third in line was a very good position to be in—I got away with murder. I was my father's favourite, no doubt about that'. There is probably a great deal more to this statement than meets the eye. Being a middle sibling is never really easy. Typically, middle siblings feel unfairly treated—as indeed, Diana later revealed that she did, while 'getting away with murder' may mean that in fact she lacked appropriate parental boundaries, controls and attention. Certainly, in later life, she showed abnormally high levels of resentment when anybody, the Royal family included, tried to control her. And was she really her father's favourite? And if so, in what sense exactly? Diana later admitted that, 'I longed to be as good as Charles in the schoolroom,', but adds quickly 'I was never jealous of him'. I strongly suspect that, although she genuinely loved them, she *was* jealous of all her siblings—of her sociable eldest sister, of her intelligent and bookish next sister, of the dead John and, of course, and principally, of her brother Charles—her father's longed-for son and heir. She may have tried, dutifully, to conceal her jealous feelings even from herself, but they were probably lurking not far below the surface. Diana once admitted 'I wasn't good at anything. I felt hopeless'. I believe that, in fact, *Diana felt the least important of all the Spencer children*. She perceived herself as living in a highly competitive situation where four children (and one little ghost) all vied for the rather sparse, elusive and erratic quantities of parental love available. For adults, feelings of love can be sustained, and even enhanced, in the absence of the loved ones, but for little children, traumatised by parental separation, this is often not possible. For Diana, her parents' absences came to signify, quite simply, that they did not love her. While the two eldest children were away at boarding school at the time of their parents' separation and so did not feel the abandonments in quite the same way, and Charles was, of course, the much wanted son, Diana was less protected from these traumas. Diana's childhood had been, as she admitted, 'very unhappy' and Charles Spencer recalls that it 'certainly lacked a mother figure'. 'Parents were busy sorting themselves out' says Diana, and she remembered 'always seeing my mother crying', adding that 'Daddy never spoke to us about it'. Her memoires indicate that by the age of fourteen she felt:

> My brother was always the one getting exams at school and I was the dropout. I couldn't understand why I was perhaps a nuisance to have around which, in later years, I perceived as being part of the (whole question of the) son, the child who died before me was a son and both (parents) were crazy to have a son and heir and there comes a third daughter. What a bore. We're going to have to try again. I've recognized that now. I've been aware of it and now I recognize it and that's fine. I accept it.

At the deepest emotional level the little Diana probably felt more indulged than wanted. Baby Diana grew up in the aftermath of the neonatal death of brother John, when Frances was made to feel that she had failed as an heir-producer, and Johnnie was feeling bitterly disappointed. Diana would later say that she felt she should have been a boy. Did she also feel that, unless John had died she would not have been born? Did she irrationally blame herself for his demise, or for the friction between her parents, their private rows, and even for their eventual divorce? As we have seen, on the surface, as far as the servants were aware, both parents appeared cheerful and fond of the little Diana. Indeed, many believed she was her father's special favourite. But were these appearances reliable? Both parents came from a class that was practised at concealing its true feelings. Did they really resent Diana, or her gender, and, unconsciously perhaps, blame her for their own unhappiness? Sometimes such feelings just cannot be helped. However desperately a kindly parent may reasonably *want* to love a child, there are sometimes stronger and more irrational feelings below the surface that run in the opposite direction. Efforts at concealment sometimes mean that appearances can be quite the opposite of the deeper truth, and a child can often sense such things.

As a child, Diana is described as a sweet and shy little girl who loved stuffed toys and animals. Nannies recall her as fearful of the dark, 'spirited' and quite obstinate. When her brother Charles was born she was three. Did she feel threatened by the arrival of the much longed-for son or did it represent a reprieve for her? Did she feel she was now let off the hook? Did her parents' half-perceived guilt, anger and disappointment over the death of baby John now disappear? Or did Diana feel consumed with jealousy when Charles was born? There are disappointingly few observations of this period in her life. Diana later recalled that she could sense the strained family atmosphere at this time. Her brother Charles has said—'As a child she was deeply unhappy. I don't remember her being a sunny child', and he has described her as 'very energetic, always on the move'.

She also, he says, had 'difficulty telling the truth'. (This is not unusual in children who find the truth too painful.) Diana would chatter constantly and, so her brother believed, try 'to get attention by being naughty'. 'She was deeply perceptive from an early age, observing everything,' a cousin recalls.

More is recorded of the period surrounding the separation of her parents, which occurred three years later when she was six, and then described as a 'delightful and 'mischievous little girl, very self-confident' and 'always laughing like her mother'. Diana's childhood can certainly be seen as a series of setbacks and rejections — several centring on her mother. Of course, these events were, in reality, more complex than simple rejections but that is how a child could perceive and feel them. The first of these perceived 'rejections' had been at her birth when she had turned out not to be the expected and long-awaited boy. We can have no idea of what impressions this may have made upon her infantile mind. Quite quickly, as we have said, the parents papered over any emotional cracks and, as far as the servants could see, it was all laughter and love again. Yet years later Diana would say: 'I was a disappointment. My parents were hoping for a boy. They were so sure I'd be a boy they hadn't even thought of a girl's name for me.'

The next perceived rejection may have been at the birth of her brother, Charles, which we have already considered. Whatever the good things in her subsequent relationship with Charles, and there were many, it would be unusual if there was not also a feeling of resentment, on her part, for the attention he must have received as the baby son and heir.

Next there were the parental rows, mainly, no doubt, about Frances' relationship with her lover Peter Shand Kydd. Children hate such scenes. Diana later recalled having overheard them from her hiding place behind the Drawing Room door. Furthermore, children can quite often misunderstand the causes of such rows and believe that they are somehow to blame. We do not know if Diana did so.

Then came the actual separation of the parents. The exact details are important. The sequence of events appears to have been as follows: in the summer of 1966 Frances had met Shand Kydd. A year later, in the late summer of 1967, Frances told the distraught Johnnie that she wanted a separation and left Althorp one day in September of that year by mutual agreement. The children had been used to their mother's trips to London but this departure may have seemed to them to be different. The next day, Diana (aged six) and Charles (aged three), together with a nanny, joined Frances at her flat in London where Frances had already enrolled both children in nearby London schools. Frances explained to her children that she and their father were having a 'trial separation'. For the next few weeks Diana and Charles continued to live with their mother in London while travelling regularly to Norfolk for weekends with their father. Johnnie then, fatefully, took legal advice. Subsequently, without telling Frances, he registered the younger children at schools in Norfolk and, at Christmas 1967 obtained a Court Order returning the two children to his custody. This legal dictat shattered what may have been, for three months, a reasonably satisfactory arrangement. Frances, unable to deal with the courts while they were closed over Christmas, had to return to London alone without the children. It was probably this second departure of their mother from Althorp, at Christmas of all times, that was experienced by Diana as abandonment. It was certainly far more devastating than the first. Diana told Andrew Morton years later that she:

> sat quietly at the bottom of the cold stone stairs at her Norfolk home, clutching the wrought iron banisters while all around her there was a determined bustle. She could hear her father loading suitcases into the boot of the car, then Frances, crunching across the gravel forecourt, the clunk of the car door being shut and the sound of a car engine revving and then slowly fading as her mother drove through the gates of Park House and out of her life.

The two youngest children were told by their mother that she would be coming back 'very soon', but they were not, according to Diana, told *why* she was leaving them. In fact, they did not see their mother again for some considerable time. Diana continued to sit on the steps, week after week, forlornly imagining her mother's return at any moment.

Frances' memories of the scene confirm the trauma. Suddenly she had found herself cut off from contact with her children and able to communicate only through lawyers. In desperation she had visited Park House in the New Year to try to see them but the door was, literally, shut in her face. She shouted their names aloud but they never heard her. 'I think it was a long time before they realised the truth, that I hadn't abandoned them', Frances told *Hello* magazine many years afterwards. In June 1968 Frances went to court with a plea to regain the custody of the children. Amazingly, she lost, due in large measure to her own mother's testimony against her. Frances had paid the penalty for defying her mother and putting in jeopardy Ruth's schemes for social advancement. Seven months later Frances filed for divorce on the standard grounds of cruelty and Johnnie counter-sued, charging her with adultery. Finally, on 15 April 1969, Johnnie was granted a Decree Nisi confirming his custody of the children.

These appalling decisions by the Courts ensured Diana's psychological destruction. Aged only six, not informed of what was really happening, Diana concluded that her mother no longer wanted her. Why was Frances not given the custody of the two young children? The answer is that Johnnie was advised by Ruth Fermoy and also by high-powered lawyers. It was a classic case of how not to end a marriage. Full credit must be given to Johnnie Spencer's solicitors for creating so much pain for the children. No doubt they did well out of it. They could have handled matters so much more humanely. These awful experiences for Diana were, in my opinion, the chief cause of her subsequent personality disorder; a disorder that over twenty years later would unsettle the Royal Family and shake the very foundations of the state.

Frances was also shattered by this experience. 'Frances was a devoted and passionate mother' a relative has said.

'She was beside herself. She was inconsolable. She cried and cried and cried. She continued crying for years.' Lady Colin Campbell comments—'the wilfulness of a husband who did not want the children for himself, but simply wanted to deprive his wife of them, was bad enough for any woman to have to swallow. But Frances also had to square away her own mother's treachery, born, as it was, of nothing more profound than snobbery and ambition.' Frances still saw a lot of her children in the ensuing years but she handled the arrangements awkwardly, allowing her offspring all too often to see the emotional distress that their visits and departures caused her, thus increasing their anxieties and feelings of guilt. Frances had a disordered personality, but such people *can* make good mothers as Diana herself was to demonstrate. The problem was that Frances was never given the chance. Diana told Morton:

> I remember mummy crying an awful lot and every Saturday when we went up for weekends, every Saturday night, standard procedure, she would start crying. On Saturday we would both see her crying. 'What's the matter, mummy?' 'Oh, I don't want you to leave tomorrow', which for a nine year old was devastating you know.

Instead of making Diana feel wanted, her mother's tears made her feel guilty. Later, Diana was angry with her mother about the tears, believing that they had a selfish and manipulative quality.

The Spencer divorce had put the needs of the father above those of his wife and children. In that regard it was typical of the worst divorces of that period. Johnnie could have insisted on doing things more humanely but he was neither an unconventional nor a brilliant man. He was shocked and angry, and was also under the influence of a powerful and vindictive mother-in-law who was, so it seems, determined that her grandchildren should grow up as Spencer aristocrats and not go off with her errant daughter to become middle class Australians or Scots.

So we have two little children, confused and frightened, abandoned at Park House, not seeing their mother for days, and maybe weeks, at a time, uncertain as to why she had left them. Diana must have wondered if it was her fault. What had she done wrong? Why did her mother not want her? Diana would have been sensitive to the aura of scandal, secrecy, shame and high emotion around her; quite typical of a divorce of that era.

Who looked after little Diana and Charles? We are told that their father was often alone in his study or out on the estate or away at meetings. He chose not to share his meals with his children and was not much of a cuddler anyway. No doubt he loved his children in his own rather hands-off way but he did not want to see too much of them, particularly when he was feeling miserable. Having had no model of an affectionate father himself he probably did not know how to relate to them in a comforting way. Nannies rapidly came and went with whom Diana did not bond, seeing them, almost immediately, not as comforters or surrogates but as her mother's usurpers. She turned her anger upon her nannies, becoming obstinate and difficult to handle. At the same time Diana began to give to others the care and cuddling that she really craved for herself. She built up a large family of cuddly toys, cosseted her guinea-pigs, took responsibility for her little brother and began to dote upon her father, following him around the house, constantly angling for his attention and, no doubt, fearful that he too might one day suddenly vanish and abandon her. After the divorce Johnnie could not bring himself to explain to the children what had happened and why their mother had gone. Perhaps he wanted them to think the worst of her. As it transpired, the parental schism proved to be absolute and Johnnie would hardly ever speak to his ex-wife Frances again for the remainder of his life.

Although Diana was made intellectually aware, in later life, that her mother had not deliberately abandoned her, she could never quite believe this nor forgive Frances for leaving the marriage. It was her mother's behaviour, after all, that had precipitated the divorce. The raw fury at feeling rejected that had burned inside Diana as a young child, had seared so deep that the anger was always to be there. Intellectual insight was not enough to cure it. The emotional wounds still festered. All this might have been softened with professional therapeutic assistance at the time, but it never was.

Touchingly, Diana tried to do this on her own, many years later, holding torrid secret meetings with her principal 'bêtes noires'—her grandmother (Ruth Fermoy), stepmother Raine and real mother Frances. With the first two she seems to have made some progress towards catharsis and reconciliation. Sadly, with her mother, she failed. At the time of Diana's death the two were hardly on speaking terms. In 1997, shortly before the end, the neurotic Frances, spouting racial venom more to have been expected from her own mother, would accuse Diana of being 'a whore' who slept with Muslim men. There are echoes here of how Frances herself had been treated by Ruth. Family patterns repeat themselves.

Five years after the severe trauma of the separation, matters somewhat improved for Diana. By the early 1970s the children were again quite regularly visiting their mother in London at weekends and sharing equally their school holidays between their parents. But what had happened in the intervening years and, in particular, the months from Christmas 1967 until, say, the end of 1969? The reports are vague. It seems possible that Diana and Charles actually went for weeks at a time without seeing Frances, virtually alone for hours, especially in the evenings, bored and without congenial companions. If so, then this was probably when further damage was done psychologically. There were, however, several more blows in Diana's childhood still to come. The first was in 1975 when the old Earl, her grandfather, died and Johnnie and his children finally moved into the daunting one hundred and twenty-one room Althorp, described by Charles as 'a chilling time warp'. Diana had loved the far smaller Park House. For children who have been emotionally traumatised by events in their lives, as Diana had been, the reliable physical presence of a familiar home is often a source of therapeutic security. Now, at the age of fourteen, she had to lose this, too. It was, she said, 'a terrible, terrible wrench'. Then, a year later, the second bombshell exploded. Her father, now the Earl, had been discovered by someone rather similar in some respects to his old ally Ruth Fermoy. When they first met Raine Legge, Johnnie's children instantly disliked her 'because we thought she was going to take Daddy away from us'. In July 1976 Raine quietly married Johnnie and set about selling off some of the family's possessions and redecorating Althorp's interior. As the only child of the romantic novelist Barbara Cartland, Raine, too, enjoyed an elegant lifestyle. Her mother's books, in which the female in distress is almost invariably rescued by her 'prince charming', had been among Diana's favourites, but this did not mean that Diana forgave Raine for taking her father away. To the contrary, initially, she heartily detested her stepmother and in 1989 finally told Raine what she thought of her: 'I've never known such anger in me ... I stuck up for Mummy', she recalled, as if Raine had somehow caused the divorce. (Was Diana trying to shift her inappropriate guilt for the divorce off her own back?) In later years, however, Diana and Raine's relationship warmed and improved. Diana had been surrounded in childhood by an extraordinary coterie of strong female characters such as Ruth Fermoy and Raine Legge with Barbara Cartland and the Queen Mother herself in the background. It is hardly surprising that she grew up to feel that all the important events in her life were being planned and manipulated by others.

Diana's memoirs

We are fortunate in having Diana's memoirs that were secretly dictated to Andrew Morton in the autumn of 1991. She was then thirty, the age at which her mother had fled the boredom of Norfolk life, and Diana herself was breaking away from her own marriage. (In many ways she was repeating her mother's life as children often do.) She still recalled the traumas of childhood all too clearly. When once asked what epitaph she wanted on her grave, the adult Diana had said: 'A great hope crushed in its infancy'. She was right. The great hope the nation felt at her fairytale wedding to Prince Charles on 29 July 1981 had indeed already been crushed out of her when she was six by the emotional blows surrounding her parents' divorce. She never recovered from these and, indeed, continued to 'act them out', as psychologists sometimes say, during the remainder of her life and, in particular, during her own marriage.

In her memoirs Diana recalls her brother's misery at the time of the separation:

> I used to hear my brother crying in his bed down at the other end of the house, crying for my mother and he was unhappy too, and my father right down the other end of the house and it was always very difficult. I never could pluck up courage to get out of bed. I remember it to this day.

Why were the two children and their father sleeping so far apart? Diana was clearly terrified of the dark and desperate. Did nobody realise her plight? There was, it seems, no motherly nanny or kindly grandmother present to do the obvious. Why, one wonders, were the grandmothers so absent? Ruth had little feeling for children but why did the revered Cynthia not step in to help? Upper class grannies, perhaps, are rarely cuddly ones. Johnnie, too, had failed to provide for his children's obvious emotional needs.

Diana feared upsetting her parents by showing favouritism to them. It was as if she felt responsible for their unhappiness, as she may well have done. Whenever she went to stay with one parent she felt guilt at leaving the other on their own. On one occasion, each parent gave her a bridesmaid's dress for the same wedding. 'To choose which one to wear was the most agonizing decision I ever had to make', she recalled. Nevertheless, Diana found a few precarious positives in her situation—'the divorce helped me to relate to anyone else who is upset in their family life'. As a child Diana did not have a social life filled with friends who could provide some of the support she craved, although she recalls being 'shunted over' to see the royals at Sandringham during her holidays: 'We hated going over there. The atmosphere was always very strange.' Her parents seemed to fall into most of the obvious traps that divorced parents can fall into, vying for the children's approval and affection, competing with each other by spoiling them with scant discipline and large presents:

> Holidays were always very grim because we had a four-week holiday. Two weeks Mummy and two weeks Daddy and the trauma of going from one house to another and each individual parent trying to make it up in their area with material things rather than the actual tactile stuff, which is what we both craved for but neither of us ever got.

Emerging patterns

At school Diana, her head still full of the divorce, failed at academic work but excelled at dancing and diving, and won the best-kept guinea-pig prize. She also liked school visits to local care homes and hospitals, and once was awarded a school cup 'for helpfulness'. Diana was also growing up to be a beauty. Later, she would play upon these strengths becoming world famous for her good works and good looks.

She would continue to give to others the care that she yearned to have for herself and, increasingly, she sought comfort in various surrogates for love, including being photographed. The latter was almost certainly because her father was for ever taking pictures of her. It was, perhaps, the nearest he could get to cuddling his daughter. Diana responded by posing obligingly. As an excellent recent biographer has recognised, photography was the way in which her father had shown his interest and, in consequence, she would always enjoy the cameras of the media. Cameras had become emblems of love for her. Of course, when the emblem turns out not to be the real thing then there is often frustration and anger. This was at the root of Diana's lifelong love/hate relationship with the paparazzi. She craved their flash bulbs but they could never, in the end, satisfy her. Deep down she still hungered for the magical food of love. Sometimes she tried food too, literally, and would binge frantically on rich foods and then, anxious not to lose her beauty, would make herself vomit it all up again, or purge herself, or irrigate colonically, or exercise desperately in order not to lose her figure.

We can see that by her late teens Diana was already showing many of the signs of a disordered personality. She feared abandonment in all her close relationships, there were swings in mood, angry spitefulness, uncalled-for kindnesses, several mild suicidal gestures, alternating over-evaluations and under-evaluations of friends, binge-eating and frequently expressed feelings of emptiness, loneliness and worthlessness. After leaving school, she tried to gain the appreciation she craved by looking after children and house-cleaning, usually for friends, and always underpaid. Yet she yearned to be a star.

The other way in which Diana was planning to fill the emotional void inside her, chiefly created by the loss of her mother at Christmas 1967, was to follow the romantic recipe provided by the Barbara Cartland novels she had so uncritically absorbed in her youth: she believed she could find true love by marrying Mr Right. Some day she would find her Prince Charming who would satisfy all her needs and staunch the agony in her heart. For years she had been saying that she sensed her destiny was to marry someone very special, perhaps even a member of the royal family.

It has been suggested that Diana's marriage to Prince Charles was, like that of her parents, a specially contrived one. The Spencers as old courtiers had always moved in the right circles to make this possible. By making Park House available to Johnnie and his children Ruth Fermoy had also guaranteed that the two families would remain in touch due to their sheer physical proximity. Was this deliberate on her part? Once Diana and Prince Charles were courting, Ruth and her friend the Queen Mother certainly took an active interest in the relationship. One explanation of Diana's nickname 'Duch' is that it alluded to a family joke that she would one day marry Prince Andrew the Duke of York and thus become a royal duchess. So the prospect of a royal marriage was already present in the Spencer family culture. The immediate trigger, or at least the catalyst for the engagement between Prince Charles and Diana was, however, the flirtatious friendship between Prince Charles and Diana's eldest sister Sarah which started in the summer of 1978 when Diana was still sixteen.

Sarah, too, was suffering from eating disorders at the time but was lively and witty. She made Prince Charles laugh. One day she had invited him over to Althorp to shoot and he had met Diana there – an apparently uncomplicated and bouncy teenager. Diana recalled – 'I remember being a fat, podgy, no make-up unsmart lady but I made a lot of noise and he (Prince Charles) liked that ... ' The Prince asked Diana to show him the picture gallery at Althorp and, as she was about to do so, 'my sister Sarah comes up and tells me to push off'. Next day Charles continued to flirt with her. 'I was just so sort of amazed' Diana remembered. 'Why should anyone like him be interested in me? And it *was* interest.' It was interest also on Diana's part. Back at school, according to one of her teachers, 'she couldn't talk about anything else ... she just seemed completely besotted, dreaming of escape, I should think, into fairytale.'

It was the beginning of Diana's greatest disaster. All her hopes for a final solution to her aching need for love were now pinned upon the unfortunate Prince Charles. Not only would he be her Prince Charming who would answer all her needs but, by getting off with him, Diana would also be victor in the fierce but covert rivalry with her similarly love-starved siblings. It would be one in the eye for Raine too who, so Diana felt, had more or less written her off. Suddenly Diana, who had hitherto felt herself to be the least significant member of the family, began to realise that she was far and away the most physically beautiful of the Spencer girls. This was to become a trump card for her. Eighteen months later Prince Charles invited Diana to his thirtieth birthday party. 'Why is Diana coming as well?' her sister had asked anxiously, in true Cinderella style. Then in July 1980 she met Charles at Petworth and, so she said, 'he was all over me again'. This was one of her favourite phrases in which she appeared to dismiss affection or sexual interest as a smothering experience, or even as an affliction like a rash. It was a way to play down its huge symbolic importance for her. Highly seductively she told the Prince that she thought he was 'lonely' and needed someone to care for him. Charles was already under pressure to get married and produce heirs and Diana certainly filled the bill. She was now nineteen, out of the top drawer and apparently a virgin. She knew already of his closeness to the Parker Bowleses but Diana's only complaint about Prince Charles at this stage, as they became engaged was that, like her father, 'there was never anything tactile about him. It was extraordinary, but I didn't have anything to go by because I had never had a boyfriend. I'd always kept them away… '

What Diana had especially missed after Christmas 1967 was being cuddled and kissed by her mother. Her father's evasive attentions had often been expressed at more than arm's length by means of photography. Now she was about to marry a man who was also unable to satisfy that 'tactile' part of her yearning. But then, she expected everything of her Prince. It was all totally unrealistic.

Analysis

I judge that by the time Diana married Charles she had already suffered at least seven serious and formative emotional blows. These were as follows:

July 1961. At birth, baby Diana upsets her parents by not being a boy. They bravely conceal their deep disappointment. Later, Diana claimed that she sensed this when an infant.

May 1964. Diana's parentally longed-for brother is born. Diana now feels she is the least important member in the family.

September 1967. Mother leaves Park House for a 'trial separation'. Initially, the children see her regularly.

Christmas 1967. Mother is obliged to leave Park House without Diana after her father secures legal custody of the children. They do not see her again for days. They are miserable and confused, and are given no explanation for their mother's disappearance. Diana construes her mother's absence as deliberate abandonment.

April 1969. Parents divorce. Father's custody of the children is confirmed. Mother re-marries and leaves to visit Australia. Diana does not see her for days or weeks at a time. After her return Frances goes to live for a while on a Scottish island (in 1972), thus making weekend visits for the children impossible.

August 1975. The family leaves the security of the much loved Park House and goes to live in the 'daunting' Althorp.

July 1976. Diana's father secretly marries Raine Legge. Diana had doted upon her father and feels betrayed by him. She angrily confronts him and slaps his face. (Much later he has a stroke and becomes 'estranged', as she puts it.)

Of all these traumas I would suggest that the events around Christmas 1967 were the most devastating for Diana. Like the other two subjects in this book it was by chance at this festive season, a particularly sensitive time for children, that she felt she had lost her mother. As in their cases, Christmas times would for ever be upsetting for her. Diana had occasional good insights and often admitted the importance of this maternal separation. It was, she said 'the most painful thing in her life, that the children weren't told why she (her mother) was leaving permanently'. In consequence, she had concluded that her mother no longer loved her.

Some of the other blows have had very little attention paid to them by biographers: the actual details of her parents' divorce, for example, and her mother's absences abroad must have all had their emotional effects. According to some biographers Frances went twice to the Courts trying to secure the custody of her children and failed on both occasions due to Frances' mother's (Ruth Fermoy's) character evidence against her. All of these events were probably experienced in the same way by little Diana, as further evidence that she was not wanted by her mother. Her father does not seem to have made much effort to disillusion her on this score. Perhaps he even encouraged his children to form this view. Taken together, the effect of all these experiences probably added up to far more than their simple sum.

They were mutually validating and reinforcing in their message: 'Your mother does not love you.'

How does a child react to such powerful evidence (as they see it) of maternal (and, indeed, paternal) rejection? Usually there are three emotions—grief due to loss, separation- anxiety and anger. We can see that Diana felt all three at the time and that these bundles of intense feelings stayed with her into adult life, often being inappropriately applied to later relationships and circumstances. What are the typical ideas and behaviours that accompany such feelings? Low self-esteem, frantic approval-seeking and sibling rivalry are some. Desperately, such people seek a commodity called 'attention'—the poor man's version of love. How does a child in such circumstances try to defend herself? By clinging to more controllable and dependent love objects that are less likely to go away—in Diana's case not only her father and younger brother but also her beloved guinea-pigs and her large collection of stuffed toys; by giving to others the love she needed for herself (e.g., to the young, the aged, the ill and most importantly to her own children); by seeking the approval of the world (by good works, for example, and through being photographed, which had special connotations of paternal love for her); by playing upon her strengths—her beauty, her dancing, her kindness to others; by becoming obsessed with the one great thing her own childhood had lacked—a stable source of tactile love, and subordinating all other events in her life to this quest. She had always identified 'other women' as somehow being a source of her misery and, as we have seen, she had shown her anger towards Raine and, earlier, to her nannies after her mother had left. (She had, paradoxically, been close to other servants, seeking their affection and approval, especially in the 'oral' comfort of the kitchen.) In later life she continued to be sensitive to any usurpers of the love that she yearned for and, eventually, Camilla (Prince Charles' confidante and future wife) would supremely fill this role. As we have seen, food and media-attention became surrogates for parental love and her bulimia can be seen in this light. Then, thanks in no small part to her acceptance of the Barbara

Cartland doctrine that all problems can be solved by a knight in shining armour, Diana saw a fairytale marriage as the answer to all her suffering, saying that she had always felt as though she was destined for some such magical romance. She said she 'knew' she was going to marry someone special. Above all, Diana was still fixated in her childhood, still trying to replay Christmas 1967 to put matters right. Lacking reliable parental love she never progressed beyond this stage of development. No hobbies, normal intellectual interests or career-challenges ever importantly featured in her life. She *was* ambitious, but for what? Being loved. Gradually, as she gained in confidence, the anger she had always felt for her loss of parental love became more apparent. As a child, afraid of further alienating her parents, she had not aimed her indignation at them (the true objects of her anger) but at unfortunate servants, girls at school or herself. Over the years her anxious control of her angry feelings had shown itself in her obsessional neatness; she loved cleaning, tidying and putting things in their proper place. Once she was married, her new position of security allowed this anger to explode upon a whole new range of scapegoats—girlfriends, courtiers, journalists, her unfortunate husband and the Royal family itself. She started to transfer her feelings for her family onto the royals, competing with Prince Charles for press attention (as she had competed for attention with her siblings), calling Prince Philip 'Pa', and then beginning to see the 'parental' royals as rejecting and mistreating her. By coincidence, and as if to encourage such transference, her husband had the same name as her brother.

Diana had expected her marriage to Charles to be the solution to all her fourteen years of pain. It never could have been. No marriage could provide a cure for emotional wounds of such depth. Her bitter disillusionment on this score further intensified her anger. So also, possibly, did her mother's almost total disappearance from her life for the two years following her marriage. Had Frances, with a sense of relief, handed over her difficult daughter to the care of Prince Charles? Once again, Diana's mother had vanished, hurtfully.

When Diana married she was an apparently virginal twenty year old. As such she was completely ill-equipped to deal with Charles' needs. He, too, was a damaged and unhappy person, pampered and yet deprived, as virtually all royals are bound to be. He had been an uncuddled and sensitive youth with a macho father, and he too now needed understanding, her understanding; but without an appropriate model, Diana had little idea of any such marital obligation. If Diana had been a sophisticated woman of the world with a stable personality she could have easily seen off the 'Camilla problem' as she later called it. Often she wrongly identified her marriage as the source of all her difficulties. But she had come to her marriage, psychologically speaking, as no more than an angry and unhappy child. Her behaviour was guaranteed to bring about exactly what she feared most. This, indeed, happened. Instead of giving to her husband the affection and understanding that he required, and which could have removed his need for Camilla, she began to bristle with the anger and suspicion of the wounded ingénue. This had the reverse effect, driving Charles back to more sophisticated and mature embraces. There was so much anger in Diana that had been bottled up throughout her childhood that occasionally it would erupt as downright maliciousness. She could be very vindictive. Diana herself recognised this. 'I can't help it,' she said, 'I've got a vengeful streak.' So when a friend once stood her up on a date, for example, she visited his home in the dead of night and poured a paste over his Alfa Romeo, ruining its paintwork. This sort of behaviour did not endear her to mature people. It was, however, all evidence of the fires burning within; of her bitter experiences of rejection as a child. With her husband she was angry and jealous, not only because of Camilla, but because of the time Charles gave to his mother, to his royal duties and even to his dogs. No doubt he also bitterly reminded her of her father and of his elusive love, and much of her anger with Prince Charles was anger that was really intended for Johnnie, just as her rivalry with him for press attention was like her rivalry with her siblings. Entering into a marriage is rather like entering into psychotherapy. Spouses must expect such transferences of feelings; wives transferring old feelings for their fathers or siblings on to their husbands, and husbands transferring their feelings for their mothers on to their wives. Wise spouses must bear patiently such undeserved feelings; they are not meant for them. Much of what Diana said about Prince Charles would have been far more appropriately targeted at members of her childhood family.

Having said all this it is, nevertheless, true that Diana had married a man who was still entangled with an old girlfriend. This would cause any woman understandable concern. How she dealt with this problem was, however, immature. As Diana so rightly observed: 'I was desperately trying to be mature about the situation but I didn't have the foundations to do it and I couldn't talk to anyone about it.' Because of her childhood experiences Diana totally lacked self-esteem and self-confidence. She felt she could not cope with 'the Camilla thing' nor with the extraordinary routines and expectations of royal life. She became 'obsessed by Camilla totally' and lost trust in her husband. She was 'desperately trying to make him proud' of her but, or so she felt, received no praise from him. Badly advised, he tried to ignore her suicidal gestures. Above all, she desperately needed encouragement, but she considered that she never received it from her new family. 'Nobody ever helped me *at all*. They'd be there to criticize me, but never to say "well done".' When the press paid her attention she felt her husband was unimpressed; indeed 'he was jealous'. As her bulimia worsened she found that her in-laws saw this condition not as a *symptom* of her failing marriage but as its *cause*. It was, of course, both. She felt her grandmother, Ruth Fermoy, had 'done a good hatchet job on me'. She probably had. The Royal Family had almost certainly fallen for the manipulations of the ruthless Ruth and were convinced that Frances was 'the baddie', that 'poor Johnnie (had) had a very rough time' and that Diana was now taking after her mother. In fact, if there was anyone in particular who was to blame for the whole dysfunctional mess in which the bemused Royal Family now found itself, it was Ruth Fermoy herself. Diana had good insights at the 'tactical' level but she failed to grasp the 'strategy' of her psychological predicament. She blamed most of her problems on those who happened to be around her at any particular moment—principally her husband, his family and his lover. She often missed the bigger picture. The roots of her problem lay not in the genuine difficulties of the marriage, nor with Charles nor Camilla, but in the disasters of her childhood.

Diagnosis

My formal diagnosis is that Diana suffered from a Borderline Personality Disorder with Bulimia. I am not *blaming* Diana for this condition. It is merely a description of how she was, which was largely a reaction to the behaviour of some of those around her in her childhood.

Personality disorders are enduring and pervasive abnormalities that cause social and occupational impairment and significant distress to the patient and to others. They are not clear-cut mental 'illnesses' like the schizophrenias, the mood disorders or the neuroses. In contrast, they are long-term and stable conditions that endure from adolescence or early adulthood and are, in a sense, part of the actual psychological structure of the person themselves. There are some ten major types of personality disorder in today's textbooks including paranoid, narcissistic, schizoid, antisocial, histrionic, obsessive-compulsive, dependent, anxious and borderline. The latter, Diana's condition, is described by the American Psychiatric Association (see Hales and Yudofsky) in the following terms:

> A pervasive pattern of instability of interpersonal relationships, self-image, and affects, and marked impulsivity beginning by early adulthood and present in a variety of contexts, as indicated by five (or more) of the following:
>
> 1) frantic efforts to avoid real or imagined abandonment. Note: Do not include suicidal or self-mutilating behavior covered in Criterion 5;

2) a pattern of unstable and intense interpersonal relationships characterized by alternating between extremes of idealization and devaluation;
3) identity disturbance: markedly and persistently unstable self-image or sense of self;
4) impulsivity in at least two areas that are potentially self-damaging (e.g. spending, sex, substance abuse, reckless driving, binge eating). Note: do not include suicidal or self-mutilating behaviour covered in Criterion 5;
5) recurrent suicidal behaviour, gestures, or threats, or self-mutilating behaviour;
6) affective instability due to a marked reactivity of mood (e.g. intense episodic dysphoria, irritability, or anxiety usually lasting a few hours and rarely more than a few days);
7) chronic feelings of emptiness;
8) inappropriate, intense anger or difficulty controlling anger (e.g. frequent displays of temper, constant anger, recurrent physical fights);
9) transient, stress-related paranoid ideation or severe dissociative symptoms.

In Diana's case the first eight of these diagnostic criteria were clearly present. Characteristic of Borderline Personality Disorder (BPD) is a severely impaired capacity for attachment. When such people feel cared for they can, paradoxically, also feel empty and lonely. Issues of care and separation are central to the condition. There are swings in mood. The sufferer's intimate perception of others alternates sharply between beneficent care-givers and cruel persecutors. Such 'disappointment reactions' with carers are common. The sufferer tends to think in simplistic 'black or white' terms. Fears of impending separation lead to rageful accusations of mistreatment and angry self-destructive actions. The sufferer lacks self-esteem and is moody, impulsive and commonly experiences intense feelings of being evil. They fear their own destructiveness and harbour doubts about their own goodness. Intimate personal relationships are often misunderstood, riddled with mistrust and fear of abandonment, and the BPD sufferer usually ends up being hurt. The lives of such people centre ultimately upon obtaining the support and approval of others; they search constantly for 'the magical food of love'.

Borderline Personality Disorders are hard to treat. A long lasting relationship of trust with a therapist may help. The therapist will have to endure and use the client's anger, transferred from the client's real feelings for the parents or others who have let them down in childhood. A structured occupation for the client that gives repeated boosts to their low self-esteem through praise and achievement may be useful. Focused cognitive and behavioural interventions have been found to be helpful, as have anti-depressant and other medications to reduce impulsivity, anger and depression.

The prevalence of BPD in the general population is estimated to be between one per cent and two per cent, being several times more noticeable in young women than in any other group. When people hear the words 'Borderline Personality Disorder' they often ask—'borderline with what?' It is a very good question that really has no definite answer. The label certainly does not imply any borderline with schizophrenia (although a similar label to indicate this was used in the past).

Various subsidiary problems sometimes occur in Borderline Personality Disorders including alcoholism, drug abuse, stealing, sexual promiscuity and eating disorders.

In Diana's case it was Bulimia Nervosa. The usual diagnostic criteria for this condition are two:

1) Recurrent episodes of binge-eating, at least twice a week over three months, characterised by consuming larger than normal amounts of food while feeling a loss of control over eating.
2) Recurrent compensatory behaviour aimed at preventing weight-gain, such as excessive exercise, misuse of laxatives, diuretics or enemas, fasting, or self-induced vomiting. (In addition, in Diana's case, there was colonic irrigation.)

Among Bulimics there is often a morbid fear of fatness, a past history of episodes of Anorexia Nervosa, and the link-ing of self-esteem to body weight and shape. Sufferers often feel anxious and shallowly depressed. Nearly all of these features applied in Diana's case. The co-existence of Bulimia with Borderline Personality Disorder is quite common and occurs in about twenty-five per cent of cases of Bulimia Neurosa.

There is no blame or shame to be attached to such conditions. The labels are merely useful descriptions of behaviour. I have recently learned that the same label has already been applied to Diana by one of Diana's most talented biographers, Sally Bedell Smith. I can only concur with her prior judgement. Although these labels can provide useful indicators for effective treatment (which Diana never actually received), they give us little understanding as to how these conditions were caused or what it actually felt like to be Diana. I have tried to explore these aspects. Current evidence suggests that BPD is caused more by childhood events than by genes. Abuse, neglect and separation have been found to be the common causes, as are parents who are inconsistent and emotionally withdrawn.

It is a characteristic of those with Borderline Personality Disorder that they are greedy. They can never be satisfied. In their desperation they grasp for more and more food, sex, approval and attention. They demand of their partners absolute and total commitment, not allowing them any other normal interests, seeing these when they occur as personal rivalries and rejections. Diana once told a friend 'her ideal man would be there for her twenty-four hours a day'. Such concerns constantly tormented her and dominated her life. Yet, before her death, Diana had accomplished many great and wonderful things—altering the public perceptions of Aids, helping to outlaw landmines, and bearing two fine sons to whom she gave all the maternal love that she considered that she herself had lacked.

Conclusions

Why was Diana's appeal to the public so great? Well, the non-Catholic Western world today lacks a female divinity, and Diana's beauty and compassion filled this empty slot. As a beautiful young woman she appealed to men as the ideal lover, and as a well-dressed and famous woman she appealed to ambitious women. As a caring woman she attracted us as the perfect mother, and as a mistreated woman she moved us as the eternal victim. Like that other wizard of mass attraction, President Bill Clinton, she also instinctively appealed to all underdogs—that's most of us! She made us feel she was on *our* side against power and authority. She was young and beautiful and the centre of attention; we could all love her or identify with her. Not only as a princess but also as the world's most famous lady, she was at the pinnacle of both the old class system and its modern replacement—the cult of celebrity.

At her death the reaction of a large section of the British public took the Royal Family by surprise. The emotion seemed out of all proportion. People were grieving more for someone they had never met than they did for a relative or friend. Why was this? Was it just the heritage of the Sixties—the abolition of the traditional British stiff upper lip and the release of feelings that had previously been suppressed? It was surely more than this. Through the extraordinary spotlight of the late twentieth-century media Diana, the apparent paragon, had become a repository for the hopes and aspirations of millions. When she died, people felt they had lost a part of themselves. By identifying with a star one becomes a star. Royalty had always, to an extent, filled this surrogate role. Over the centuries royals and celebrities have traditionally been figures of soap-opera in the national mind. For those with dull, despairing or dissatisfied lives such soap-operas provide a pleasant escape from reality. Through the gods and goddesses of religion, and the heroes and heroines of mythology, not to mention the gossip columns of the modern tabloid press, and stories of celebrity and royalty, such escapism has always been a way to deaden the pains of living.

Diana was, of course, not as she was perceived. Far from enjoying her position as the world's leading lady, she was utterly miserable. She still felt rejected. Principally, Diana blamed her mother for the parental divorce and made the infantile mistake of seeing it as a deliberate abandonment of the children by her mother. 'Mummy decided to leg it' Diana said years later, matching her father's description of her mother as 'the bolter'. In fact there is no evidence that Frances had ever intended to leave her children behind her. Usually, even in 1968, the Courts gave custody to mothers, but this did not happen in this case. That was the turning point. The extraordinary Court decisions were the fateful blows that determined the future of Diana's unhappy life.

Diana had also been unlucky in her choice of grandparents, two of the three alive in her childhood being abnormal. These lacked warmth and produced parents for Diana who were insecure, unrounded and unwise. Both of her parents made mistakes. Johnnie was weak and withdrawn from his children; Frances was turbulent and too emotional. Later, both parents, unconsciously perhaps, used the children as weapons against their ex-spouses. Both parents competed in showing their affection for their children by piling material presents upon them and by failing to control them with normal discipline. Warmth, understanding and structure were often lacking. Diana grew up, in consequence, somewhat wayward, reacting very badly to subsequent attempts at control by courtiers and others. The Buckingham Palace culture of self-discipline was anathema to her and she wrongly interpreted it as a lack of love and concern for her children and herself, accusing Prince Charles, for example, of being a 'bad father' when he failed to be with his sons due to his royal obligations and sense of duty. Her own parents had provided too few such disciplines for her. Because of her childhood experiences she saw rejections and abandonments everywhere, even where none were intended.

Although Diana's father had tried to reassure her, deep down Diana was not certain that either of her parents had really loved her. When Johnnie had a stroke in 1978, Diana commented 'he couldn't talk because he had a tracheotomy so he wasn't able to ask where his children were'. By saying this Diana is trying to explain away his apparent lack of concern for her at this time of crisis. She fears he was not *really* interested in her. After his second marriage her beloved father became more than ever distant from her and when she complained in 1991 about Raine's sale of family possessions from Althorp, her father had hit back at her quite hard. Diana was mortified by this. Later they tried to make up this quarrel.

Approval, respect, attraction, admiration and friendship are especially valuable later, but for a young child it is the cuddling that is needed. As we have seen, she felt that Prince Charles, just like her father, did not sufficiently cuddle her. She always remembered her father's absences—his 'lonely silences', while she sat alone, hugging herself, her brother sobbing himself to sleep. Her father's love had been difficult to catch onto and secure. It was certainly not 'tactile'. Perhaps a little embarrassed by all her emotion, he had tried to keep his distance from her. Yet, before the divorce, her mother *had* cuddled her.

The separation in 1967 had also occurred at an age when Diana might have been, quite naturally, passing through an Oedipal stage in her own development, (see Glossary) and partially aware that she and her mother were female rivals for her father's attention. When she notes that it was her father (and not her mother herself, nor the servants) who loaded up her mother's suitcases as she finally departed Althorp, is Diana telling us that she saw this as her father's ejection of her mother, perhaps in her favour? Did she half believe that it was her father who was sending her mother away? Did her mother also feel this? Was there, in fact, not only guilt on Diana's part but also jealous anger felt by her mother? Oedipal feelings often go both ways; it is not just the children, but also the parents, who can have them. Fathers can feel great jealousy of 'mother's boy' sons, and mothers of 'Daddy's darling' daughters. Did this apply in Diana's case? Perhaps there is just the possibility that Johnnie, probably unwittingly, used this to hurt Frances after their separation. This would help to explain Diana's constant guilt and anxiety over favouring one parent or the other. But it also means that Diana sensed or suspected that her father's apparent interest in her was a fake;

that his intermittent shows of affection had merely been a device to get his own back on his ex-wife by making her feel jealous of Diana.

In the 1980s, Diana hoped that Prince Charles would be the cuddly ideal father figure she had never had, after 'losing' her actual father to Raine. Love-starved children often invent such romantic ideals. Sadly, Prince Charles turned out also to be a non-cuddler and to have his own Raine. 'I hoped for a husband to look after me', Diana once said. 'He would be the father figure to me, he would support me, encourage me, say "well done" or "that wasn't good enough". I didn't get any of that. I couldn't believe it!'

Diana has been accused of courting the media rather as she courted her father's photography. Of course she did and, overall, she did it well, and for the same reasons. Her manipulations of non-media people appear naïve in comparison. Desperate to raise her own approval of herself, and finding that Prince Charles was not able to provide the magical food of love in the huge amounts she yearned for, she began to play to the gallery. The world at large would have to provide that love for her. So, through the media she paraded not only her beauty but also her good works as if to say, 'Look! Am I not worthy of being loved?' When she felt guilty about such ulterior and selfish motives, she did some good works very privately, punishing herself with long nocturnal journeys to visit Aids sufferers and others, trying to prove to herself that she was *really* good. Much of her charitable work was with children and some of her public speeches on child-care are full of half-hidden personal references: 'hugging has no known harmful side-effects' she said once and, on another occasion—'we must all play our part in making children feel valued,' thus 'helping our children to face life as stable adults'. Diana had these occasional insights into the origins of her own emotional instability, but no-one arranged for her to have the highly skilled psychological assistance that she so desperately needed. Was this a failing in our system? It is certainly a feature of British society that high quality psychotherapy is hard to find and that families of any sort—not just royal ones—have little understanding as to how to obtain such assistance.

Towards the end of her marriage Diana increasingly displayed her misery and aloneness to the public. She now felt she needed the *world*'s understanding, approval and compassion. She was upset by the occasional media hostility that she later received but this only intensified her obsession with the press. Her relationship with the media began to take the place of relationships with friends. Not far below the surface was still her sense of worthlessness and yet deeper, perhaps, her guilt for not being a boy and even for being a cause of her parents' divorce. Maybe she hated herself for all this, and for all the anger she knew she had inside her. Near the end of her life Diana became quite paranoid suspecting, rather melodramatically, that 'they', presumably the Royal Family, were out 'to get her'. She feared, Lord Mischon said, that 'efforts would be made, if not to get rid of her, be it by some accident in her car, such as pre-prepared brake failure or whatever ... at least to see that she was so injured or damaged as to be declared "unbalanced".' She also believed she was being bugged and her telephones monitored. Raine Spencer, giving evidence to the official inquest in December 2007 stated that Diana 'was obsessed about the idea of accidents ... that something was going to happen to her'.

To an extent, this was Diana's own anger and self-destructiveness being projected onto her external world. By the mid 1990s Diana was despairing and desperate. Nothing, so it seemed to her, could rid her of her feelings of rottenness and misery. Whatever she had tried—good works, marriage, celebrity, quack therapies, bulimia, lovers—had failed to give her any lasting respite from her psychological pain. There was, in consequence, a part of her that probably wanted to end it all. After the apparent collapse of the love affair with Hasnat Khan she had almost had enough of life. That is possibly why, only a week after her last troubled meeting with Khan, despite her expressed fears of a contrived car accident, she failed to strap on her seat belt in the back of the Mercedes in Paris. If she had worn it, so experts have testified, she would have lived.

The adult Diana still felt the desperately low esteem and the cravings for approval and appreciation that she had felt when young and, as she grew older, the anger and vindictiveness she might have more appropriately expressed to her parents for the hurts they had inadvertently caused her, she now peppered on to those around her. To pin so much unrealistic hope upon her marriage, and then to find infidelity, was the ultimate shock to her already damaged personality. Like many children who are short of parental love she had invented a fantasy of ideal love that, in her case, she believed she would find in matrimony. The reality of her marriage dashed these hopes. But her disappointing marriage and the vagaries of the Buckingham Palace subculture were merely the triggers for, and not the causes of Diana's dysfunctional behaviour. These causes were back in 1967 when little Diana had believed that her mother had abandoned her. She was already a deeply damaged person long before Prince Charles began to show any interest in her. Diana's childhood had made her obsessed with a craving for reliable parental love and this had assumed an overwhelming importance for her. She had learned that she could trust neither of her parents to be there when she needed them. Diana had naïvely thought her royal marriage would answer all these problems but, because it shattered her fairytale hopes, it only made them worse.

Some final thoughts

Many wonder whether Diana had found her true love in Dodi Fayed. I very much doubt it. Friends have said that her relationship with him was chiefly an attempt to make Hasnat Khan jealous and to rekindle his interest. Anyway she was, by her middle thirties, so stuck in her ways emotionally that there could be for her no Prince Charming with all the answers. Indeed, during the 1990s she had adopted another familiar and futile technique with which Borderline Personality Disorders try to quench their craving for love;

she was taking lovers quite frequently. There had been a number in the few years before her death.

Hasnat Khan was certainly the nearest to being a psychologically worthwhile choice among her male friends. He came across as a mature, serious and reliable man. As a surgeon he was also, she probably felt, a 'good' man, someone whose work she could respect far more than the lives of the superficial polo-playing and fox-hunting set she had previously known. He would, she thought, be 'a good father' for her. They could do good works together. He was also, as a Muslim, an outsider and so someone who engaged her own sense of caring. Understandably, perhaps sensing her dysfunctional nature, Khan backed away from full commitment. He feared, he said, the high levels of publicity that would ensue.

Her only real hope for tranquility of mind would have been in her continuing role as a successful mother and, perhaps, in some structured job as an international philanthropist or ambassador. In this way she might have raised her self-esteem more securely and begun to accept herself more fully. She had started to form friendships, too, with older 'motherly' women and this was a more rewarding tactic. After many years of achievement, being a good mother herself, and growing maturity, she might at last have settled. Perhaps in later middle age she might eventually have found the mature and stronger man who could love her unconditionally and satisfy her, by then, reduced cravings for the 'magical food of love'. Maturity, or even the passage of time itself, can mellow conditions such as hers.

Could she have been treated for her problems? Well, of course, she *was* psychiatrically treated but, quite rightly, we have not been told about the details. Maybe this treatment helped her in small measure. Too often, however, Diana resorted, pathetically, to 'alternative' therapies. Treatment itself, sensible or zany, effective or not, became another love-surrogate for her. The treatment of Bulimia is, in fact, awkward, and the successful treatment of Borderline Personality Disorder decidedly difficult. The wounds are usually too deep and too long-standing by the time that adulthood has been reached. Far earlier Family Therapy could have helped, but it was probably now too late. Yet, shortly before she died, Diana's relationship with her mother was so raw and turbulent that some strong therapeutic intervention, working with both women together, might still have been effective. Their anger with each other had now bubbled to the surface; Diana's anger at what she still perceived as her mother's abandonment, and her mother's anger at Diana for not being able to understand what had really happened all those years ago. Maybe Frances was also still angry at the attention given to Diana by Johnnie. Frances probably felt she had had a miserable life and was upset that she had received so little understanding from her daughter. In her last months Diana had become so angry that she was projecting much of this fury onto others and seeing plots and conspiracies all about her. Egged on by the visions of some of her pet psychics, Diana even believed, as we have seen, that members of the Royal Family were trying to kill her. The divorce was upsetting her far more than she had expected.

Unlike children with parents who die (such as Adolf Hitler and Horatio Nelson) or otherwise *totally* desert them, Diana had had parents who were still alive and present for some of the time. But this had meant that, unlike an orphan, she could not completely 'start again' and find other parent figures as Horatio did. It was specifically Johnnie and, in particular, Frances, that she still needed so desperately. Nobody else would do. The Borderline Personality Disorder sufferer does not, for this reason, grow up cold, unable to bond at all, or as a continuously angry psychopath determined to punish the world. No, Diana remained sensitive and longing for steady parental love. After all, her parents had never hated her, hit her, nor *entirely* rejected her. No, they had expressed their love intermittently with photography and presents, but had then disappeared! Emotionally-speaking, they had come and gone unreliably throughout her life. This kept Diana waiting and yearning, too insecure in childhood to express her anger to them directly in case they went away again.

Experimental psychologists for many years have known that occasional and unreliable rewards are far more addictive than rewards that are reliable. As a child, Diana had tried many ways to secure her parents' affection and attention, but she had only received these rewards intermittently. That is why she had become so addicted to her yearning for love, and had never been able to grow out of such childish behaviour. Poor Diana was stuck, still performing the same sort of attention-seeking tricks she had used as an unhappy six-year-old; still dissatisfied, still hurt, and still angry. Because the Borderline Personality Disorder child has never felt secure parental love she does not develop into a normal being, secure enough *not* to be constantly obsessed with the quest for parental love. Diana was like this. She was not a normally secure person—she was a gaping emotional wound. As a result of her agony, her appetite for love was abnormal and gargantuan. She needed it in huge dollops, and with utter reliability and unconditionality over some considerable length of time, if ever she was going to close that wound. Working with a young Diana and her mother together in joint family therapy might have helped to resolve some of Diana's misperceptions of her mother as someone who had abandoned her. Diana's vast anger on this score could then have been dissipated, or expressed and handled safely, and mother and daughter could have 'gone back' over twenty years to begin to rebuild their shattered relationship.

Diana did not yearn for celebrity in order to validate a doting parent's high opinion of her. In her case, even more than with Adolf and Horatio, fame was a substitute for parental love, accentuated by her childhood rivalry for attention with her siblings, and by her father's idiosyncratic habit of using photography as a surrogate for affection. As other solutions to her misery failed—marriage, bulimia, strange therapies—Diana increasingly relied upon celebrity to boost her sagging self-esteem. She became dependent upon the media, often manipulating and tantalising them to maintain their interest. If she could not have her mother's steady and enduring love she would have the affection of the world instead. Appearing not to want the media's attention was one device she used to preserve it, and to ensure that they continued to revere her. She convinced those around her that she hated the media but it was a far more complex relationship than that. Playing a dangerous and desperate game with the paparazzi in Paris, it all would end in tragedy.

In his moving speech at Diana's funeral, her brother Charles Spencer fondly described his sister as 'unique, complex ... and beautiful'. She was, indeed, all three of these things.

Sources

Bedell Smith, Sally, *Diana: The Life of a Troubled Princess* (London: Aurum Press, 1999)

Bradford, Sarah, *Diana* (Harmondsworth: Penguin, 2006)

Brown, Tina, *The Diana Chronicles* (London: Century, 2007)

Campbell, Lady Colin, *The Real Diana* (London: Arcadia Books, 2004)

Daily Telegraph, 13 December 2007; 15 January 2008; 4 March 2008; 8 April 2008

Hales, Robert E. and Yudofsky, Stuart C., eds, *Essentials of Clinical Psychiatry*, 2nd edn (Washington & London: American Psychiatric Publishing Inc., 2004)

Hello! magazine, 15 June 2004 comment on *Frances Shand Kydd*

Kernberg, Otto, *Borderline Conditions and Pathological Narcissism* (New York: Jason Aronson, 1975)

Andrew Morton: *Diana – Her True Story : In Her Own Words* (London: Michael O'Mara Books Ltd., 1997)

Merritt, Mike, *Scotland on Sunday*, 2 October 2002

Princess Diana Exhibition, Kensington Palace, November 2007

Spencer, Charles, *The Spencer Family* (London: Viking, 1999)

Epilogue

This trilogy consists of psychological interpretations based upon well-known and often highly respected biographies and memoirs. My three subjects all lost their mothers when they were young. This trauma, perhaps the most horrendous loss that can befall any child, proved, in every case, to be a crucial event that continued to affect them throughout their lives. Their consequent insecurities made all of them crave and find celebrity. Nelson and Hitler had further features in common, both of them unconsciously and symbolically striving to protect their long dead mothers and to rescue them from danger. Nelson did this by defeating Napoleon at sea and Hitler by launching the Second World War. Both were in the business of symbolic mother-protection (hence motherland-protection), and both fell for women they had symbolically rescued from the enemy; the enemy for Nelson being France and for Adolf 'father'. We have gone through the evidence for this and I believe it stands up. Diana, whose maternal loss was psychological but not physical, chose the world as her parental surrogate and caused it to fall in love with her. It was these three people's differing reactions to the trauma of maternal loss that dominated the formation of their extraordinary careers. All three were driven by the largely unconscious fantasies that this loss generated.

Modern theories of personality have tended to isolate just five principal factors, all linked to underlying brain systems—neuroticism, extraversion, conscientiousness, agreeableness and imagination. All three of my subjects rate highly on agreeableness and appear average on extraversion. On neuroticism Nelson was probably average whereas Hitler, and Diana especially, were higher. Nelson differed from the others in being highly conscientious, whereas Hitler was by far the most imaginative and creative intellectually. All three were charmers who could show flashes of hypomanic charisma. They are all examples of those who have lusted for fame and found it; in Nelson's case and Hitler's because they were narcissists, and in Diana's because she felt unwanted. In the first two cases they did so to confirm their mothers' high opinions of them, and in the latter to find 'the magical food of love'.

Four psychological features

These studies underline several peculiar yet fundamental truths about human nature. The first is that when faced by an environmental pressure of a psychological sort a child usually reacts in one of two quite opposite directions: either he gives in to the pressure or he reacts against it. So if a parent, for example, orders a lazy child to work harder at school the child either does so or, paradoxically, becomes even 'lazier'. There is an unpredictability about which path will be chosen; compliance or rebellion. To make matters even more dubious in the eyes of the sceptical lay person, when faced with the psychologist's interpretation of such behaviour, the child may show elements of *both* reactions, becoming both more studious and less so at the same time! He becomes, in the jargon, *ambivalent* on the subject of schoolwork—or about love or career or whatever issue is at stake. Cynics can therefore be forgiven for thinking that the psychologist always wins. Whichever direction the child goes the psychologist can find an explanation in terms of some pressure, usually parental. I agree that psychologists can appear to be slippery in this way. Nevertheless, having worked with teenagers and their families for years I am certain that parental influences are of paramount importance in shaping the behaviour of children and of the later adult, causing them to go one way or another.

The second fundamental feature of human development that often gets psychologists into trouble is its frequent jerkiness. A child may suddenly switch from one type of behaviour to another quite different (indeed, often opposite) way of behaving. A fearful little boy may one day become exceptionally brave; a cruel little girl may become a compassionate one, or a boy who is jealous and spiteful towards his younger sibling may, overnight, become kindly and protective. Personalities often develop in a series of such sudden jerks. People are entitled to remain sceptical about this, but there it is.

A third feature of human behaviour is that it is frequently unconsciously motivated. The agent herself is partially or wholly unaware of why she does things. Sceptics find this view particularly annoying and so do some scientists. As a scientist myself I understand this annoyance. But, in fact, modern neuro-science strongly reinforces the importance of the unconscious and I am convinced, having worked with so many clients over the years, that motives that are unconscious do indeed frequently play a crucial role in shaping behaviour. So, although many of the day-to-day actions of our three subjects were determined by obvious and fairly conscious motives, and all three had a grasp of reality, from a deeper level the swell of their unconscious emotional pathologies would determine the overall course of their lives, occasionally bursting through the surface to create moments of madness.

Another irritating habit of psychologists is our feeling that personalities—and hence behaviour patterns—are largely established in childhood, and this is a fourth great truth. After the end of the twenties at least, little changes. People 'mellow' or grow cantankerous, of course, and moods and mental health may change but, on the whole, attitudes, values, and habits stabilise quite early in life. Some historians do not like this notion. As good intellectuals they prefer to believe that great books, political movements and new ideas can alter the behaviour of people, even in adulthood. Of course they can, but not excessively. I believe that in this respect historians tend to over-value the power of 'reason'. In fact most adult behaviour contains large slices of irrationality and childishness.

Interpretation

Much of the difficulty in psychobiography is in the *selection* of biographical facts of particular psychological importance from the vast amounts of data available. Judging such salience depends, to an extent, upon clinical experience. There are, however, some features of evidence that can suggest significance; for example, whether such evidence is often repeated, if it ties in with other clues, whether it is too strenuously denied or grossly distorted in memory, if it glaringly stands out from its context ('like a sore thumb') or if it is marked by idiosyncrasy. When exploring psychodynamics, one often discovers that attitudes, feelings and behaviours are created not by one cause but by many. As Freud realised, it is when several psychological causes coincide that they become particularly potent. So when a psychodynamicist, such as myself, produces two or three reasons for the same psychological event this is not necessarily sloppy thinking; such reasons are not competing alternatives, they are complementary and additive.

Understanding the mind is still not an entirely scientific process. Scientific psychology is advancing steadily but it has not yet got there. Upsetting though it may be for the ultra-cautious reader, we are not yet able to understand our subjects entirely by the scientific method. So I have had to resort quite often to intuition and speculation both in the testing of evidence and in reaching conclusions. Sorry, but there it is. The scientific method entails the formulation of hypotheses that must be falsifiable, and the testing of such hypotheses against the evidence. This is almost exactly what happens in psychotherapy. The therapist presents the patient with a succession of hypotheses about their behaviour and challenges the patient (or his biographer) to falsify them. This has been my approach to understanding Hitler, Nelson and Diana. It is not rigorous science but it is an interesting parallel.

Readers may have found examples of such interpretative procedures in the previous pages that will upset them. I hope they will suspend their irritation for a while and contemplate that perhaps there is *some* truth in what I have suggested. Sometimes, of course, I may have been entirely wrong. Human beings are among the most complicated known structures in the universe and so it is unsurprising that they are often difficult to comprehend. I have done my best.

Celebrity

To achieve great celebrity (unless it is thrust upon us) one must want it so desperately that all else pales into nothingness. We have found, in these three cases, that to have such an intensity of yearning was a sign of grievous childhood injury. What drives our current twenty-first-century obsession with celebrity? It seems to be based upon a basic urge to be noticed. There is also the corresponding natural tendency to be attracted to, and interested in, those who *are* noticed. Each age and culture handles fame differently. The Greeks and Romans carried the cult to extremes. For the Romans the route to celebrity was chiefly through military success, whereas for the Greeks there were several routes—wisdom, athletic prowess, oratory and literary success being among them. Claiming to be a messiah or a preacher was a characteristic of ancient Middle Eastern and Indian celebrity and, in the European Middle Ages, saintliness and piety joined royalty as the means to attaining it. With the Renaissance, alternative routes proliferated, first with a respect for political power and wealth, and then with virtuosity in the arts and, finally, in the sciences. By the seventeenth century European cultures offered a score of different ladders to celebrity. Yet, at this time, the brakes began to be applied. Nonconformist Christian traditions started to preach humility and to caution against the sin of pride. For three hundred years class systems overtook the cult of fame as touchstones for human esteem and status. In British culture fame was chiefly limited to those who were adjudged to be high-minded either as statesmen, patriots, Empire-builders, philanthropists, artists, warriors or aristocrats. Seeking to be noticed for the sake of being noticed was despised, and modesty, false or genuine, was regarded as a virtue. In America, the class system was different and obvious wealth replaced aristocracy as a means to celebrity.

It was in the middle of the twentieth century that fame began to reassert itself due, most probably, to the spread of wealth, pop music and sports, and to the proliferation of the mass media. More people had the material means and time to indulge their natural yearning to be noticed, just at the time when mass literacy, radio and television, not only provided the channels through which fame could flow in unprecedented quantities, but rapaciously demanded a continuously expanding supply. These days, very little by way of real achievement is required before the ever-hungry media train their spotlights upon new, alleged, celebrities. A few, desperate for attention, resort to the notoriety of scandal, crime and even of self-destroying terrorism.

The three subjects of this book were all virtuosi in the techniques of celebrity. For each of them fame in itself was a major spur, although never the sole *director* of their actions. They all had additional motivations. Horatio Nelson chose the traditional route to fame through military success and valour. Adolf Hitler gained fame and power through his own oratory. Princess Diana found celebrity through royalty, beauty and good works. Whereas Nelson had to promote his own fame by describing his victories in letters to his friends, beseeching them to leak them to the press, Hitler had the advantage of employing one of the most able of all 'spin doctors', Dr Joseph Goebbels, who brilliantly exploited the latest channels of communication – radio and film; indeed Adolf was a significant innovator in techniques of self-promotion that have subsequently been used by many other celebrities. Diana, inadvertently trained by her father to do so, accentuated her fame through the lenses of the media, for sixteen years carrying on a flirtatious and seductive love-affair with the cameras of the world. All three of my subjects were, indeed, superstar celebrities, and not least because their wounded childhoods had inflated their natural desire for fame into a sickness. All three sought celebrity but only

Adolf sought power even more than celebrity. Unlike Horatio and Diana, Adolf had always been assured of his mother's affection, and it was the outcome of the struggle with his father that was uncertain; thus the achieving and wielding of power was for him the overriding objective.

Psychology and history

Some historians argue that individuals do not make history and that major events are caused only by combinations of economic, physical and cultural forces, and by chance itself. Of course these things are important. They were important in the late eighteenth century when England was expanding her empire and her navy to protect her interests against France. In all probability Nelson, for example, would not have been heard of today if there had been no Napoleonic wars. But he survived all the fearful risks he took as a young man and, through a series of victories at sea, forced Napoleon to abandon his plans to invade England. Would any other British admiral have done the same? Others were equally good tacticians but did they inspire their men as Nelson did? Did they show that extraordinary motivation that drove Nelson to win the battle of Copenhagen rather than follow orders to retreat? Were they driven by the same determination utterly to destroy his enemy that Nelson showed at the Nile? Would they have taken the triumphant risks that Nelson took at the Battle of Cape St Vincent and, finally, at Trafalgar? In every case the answer is negative. In consequence, the morale of the French navy would not have been so utterly crushed. All these achievements were effects not of economics nor training nor accident but of the strange psychology of Horatio Nelson.

Economic, physical, political and cultural factors were important, too, in Germany in the 1930s when the Great Depression, combining with the continuing reaction against the humiliation of 1918, the fear of Bolshevism, and the general disorder and insecurity in Germany, created a situation in which millions of Germans longed for strong leadership and some sense of national pride and purpose.

Adolf Hitler happened to be in the right place at the right time. But by 1932 the Nazis had never received more than thirty-seven per cent of the national vote and it was only the miscalculations of conservative politicians, eager to destroy the new German democracy, that allowed Hitler to be appointed Chancellor in January 1933. They underestimated him, believing that he would not last long. They were wrong. Adolf's personal fanaticism ensured he would secure his position and put into effect the crazy ideas, influenced by his own psychodynamics, that he had already outlined years earlier in *Mein Kampf*—and the whole world would suffer in consequence. Adolf's peculiar psychology played a key part. If he had been a more 'ordinary' politician, his single-mindedness and ruthlessness would have been lacking and Germany, with economic recovery, might have followed a far more pacific path.

Diana was, of course, unlikely to have become the world's leading female celebrity unless she had married Prince Charles and been stunningly beautiful, and at a time when the visual mass media, tabloids and television, were at a peak of their popularity and power. But it was the peculiarities in her psychological make-up that gave her story the elements of paradox, hope and tragedy that ensures her legendary status.

All three of my subjects were 'driven' people and it was this exceptional motivation that made them and their achievements so extraordinary. In all three cases psychology was an essential ingredient in the determination of events. In history, psychology matters.

Culture

However important relationships are within the childhood family in explaining the actions of adulthood, these always occur in the context of a particular culture. (By 'culture' I mean the customs, attitudes and values of the time and place, to which most people conform and by which all are affected.) Nelson was living in the mannered, patriotic, class-structured world of Georgian England where behaviour was still explained in terms of classical and Christian virtues. Hitler was growing up in the authoritarian, racist, nationalistic, militaristic and sexually inhibited world of late nineteenth-century Austro-Germany. Diana, on the other hand, was a child in the changing world of 1960s Britain that was still class-conscious but was also increasingly a society where culture was being redefined by television and celebrity. All three were children in times of rapid cultural change. Old values were under attack and revolutions were in the air.

How far should the psycho-biographer take culture into account in trying to produce a full and rounded explanation for their subjects' behaviour? We can see that Nelson in his conventional religious attitudes, his patriotism and support for monarchy, was very much a child of his times. He stood for the cultural status quo. Diana, although born into a traditional upper class family was far more a product of the new 'sixties' culture; she conformed to some of the outward trappings of class while going along with the new egalitarian attitudes and liberal values of the 'swinging' sixties and seventies. Hitler's interaction with his contemporary culture is far more problematical; to a considerable extent his appalling behaviour can be seen as merely the expression of what was already a pernicious culture. Hitler's ideas were certainly crazy—but then millions of people have ideas that are equally confused. He was not, however, a true psychopath, nor an obvious sadist, nor psychotic; he was only slightly unusual psychologically. How, then, could he cause the deaths of forty million men, women and children? To a large extent it was because he was part of a (Germanic) culture that, at that time, accepted that racial pride, war and ruthlessness were not only normal but also glorious things. Furthermore, it was a culture that looked up to those in authority and believed in the concept of 'the genius' hero who would rescue Germany from its present parlous state. Undoubtedly Austro-German culture after the defeat and ignominy of 1918 was in an extraordinary condition. The collapse of the Austro-Hungarian Empire and the failure to establish a German Empire to rival that of Britain had bred a spirit of angry nationalism. Unemployment, poverty and hurt pride had whipped up support for traditional bellicose *völkisch* attitudes and values. Furthermore, the German belief in genius and respect for leadership allowed Hitler to gain a degree of personal power that would have been hard to attain in some other European countries. In every society there are eloquent narcissists and racial bigots but they do not cause the sort of damage that Hitler caused. It was unfortunate that a mass culture seeking vengeance and aggrandisement permitted the rise to power of such a man. Once in power, using the driving force of his personal psychopathology, he then proceeded to amplify these worst features of current German culture. Hitler needed, for purely personal reasons and with a burning intensity, what a growing part of German society was already wanting for more general reasons.

What other evidence is there that World War II was largely a sign or symptom of one man's mental peculiarity? Well, the oddness of Hitler was revealed by his insatiability. If he had stopped his aggression after the invasion of Czechoslovakia he might have ruled for another thirty years. If he had not attacked Russia nor provoked America the Third Reich might still be dominating Europe to this day. To have provoked two of the world's greatest military powers unnecessarily, as he did, was utter foolishness. Hitler's irrationality became increasingly apparent as the years went by. This was because inside his foreign policy was a nucleus of individual pathology—*Hitler's interminable struggle with his father*. Furthermore, like most personality disorders Hitler showed a compulsion to repeat his mistakes, and this was the worm of madness at the heart of Nazism that ultimately destroyed it; he had to keep attacking, refusing any compromise or tactical retreat. Germany's lust for conquest might have been satisfied by 1940 but Hitler's was not. He could not stop.

So we can see very clearly with Hitler (and also, to a lesser extent, with Nelson) how one man's personal psycho-pathology, the individual's dreams and fantasies, can slide insidiously into the existing manifestations of a nation's culture, energizing and inflaming them. The Nazi leaders all shared the same anti-semitic, patriotic and *völkisch* culture, but as individuals they showed some psychological differences. Hitler was the extreme antisemitic fantasist and fanatic and the only true leader after Röhm had been disposed of. All the rest were mere followers. Göring was a drug addict wallowing in narcissistic foibles to stave off his depressions, and the club-footed Goebbels an intelligent nobody who was so pleased to have become a somebody. Another nobody, Himmler, was a romantic and wimpish cultist; one of the few of the top brass to have been properly educated. He was neither a true sadist nor an anti-semitic fanatic; he was, however, pathologically ambitious. He lectured the SS against gratuitous cruelty but excused the Holocaust on the grounds of efficiency and necessity. Heydrich, the concert-pianist failure, was the nearest to Hitler in terms of fanaticism and anti-semitism. All these men had found personal advancement and a meaning to their frustrated lives through following Hitler and in striving desperately for his approval. It was a gang of nobodies. None of the top Nazis were true cultural rebels; all were conformists to the existing *völkisch* side of German culture. Yet, as in Hitler's case, individual psychopathologies played an essential part in providing the drive and persistence that were necessary in establishing these norms as the foundations of the Reich.

Two mechanisms of excess

If Germany had not been humiliated in 1918 Hitler would never have been heard of; he would probably have frittered his life away as an impoverished and embittered crank. How then, once in power, could he have caused so much misery in the world? Two psychological mechanisms were in play here. The first was Hitler's lack of empathy for his enemies – the Jews, the Bolsheviks, foreigners, indeed those outside his circle of associates. He lived in such a world of fantasy that the real world was sometimes unreal to him. People beyond the range of his direct sensory experience were mere ciphers in his plans; he did not fully imagine their sufferings. Yet he was not an insensitive man. Even if there were sadistic and spartan streaks in his character they do not explain the full scale of the horrors for which he was responsible; it was his lack of empathy for those beyond his immediate circle that made these possible.

Adolf never saw, and rarely wanted to know, the awful details of the actual effects of his fantasies upon other individuals. Ideas meant more to him than realities. In the latter years of the war he very rarely visited a frontline, never toured a concentration camp and refused to visit bombed German cities. He became in many ways, completely out of touch. After 1943 he hardly ever saw what the war's disasters looked like at first hand and, appropriately perhaps, he travelled on trains with blacked-out windows through which he could see nothing. He never allowed the natural restraining influences of compassion, that even he possessed, to counteract the awful repercussions of his orders. Hitler had very considerable powers of empathy (which he mostly showed to women) but he deliberately switched these off and kept them untriggered when it came to the masculine pursuit of war. The second psychological mechanism was the familiar one that allows most normal people to do what they are told to do by figures of authority; this rule applies even in far less authoritarian cultures than that of the Reich. These two principles, which we can call the 'out-of-touch' principle and the Milgram principle (the latter named after Stanley Milgram who demonstrated its power scientifically), explain how so much suffering can be caused by one leader. Out-of-touchism, when combined with obedience to authority, accounts for much of the cruelty of the world. Those in command are out of touch with the suffering they are ordering while those directly causing it feel they are merely obeying orders.

Maternal loss

This trilogy is much about maternal love—the most important emotional nutrient for any child. Most of us need to have felt that our mothers loved us when we were little. We need it like young seedlings need the warmth of the sun. Yet many things can go wrong either with the quality of that love or its duration. The nature of its loss, too, can vary. With Nelson we have a son who was probably his mother's favourite but her love seems to have been *conditional* upon her little boy's daring behaviour; when his loss came it was sudden, total and at the tender age of nine. Hitler was another mother's favourite but her love for him was *unconditional* and the loss came after some weeks of illness during which the eighteen year old Hitler had nursed his mother with utter tenderness. Princess Diana, on the other hand, had never been quite sure how much her mother had loved her; the loss, when it came, was not through death but apparent abandonment when she was aged only six. For all three the longing to discover or rediscover their mothers' perfect love would prove to be the dominating principle in their lives. Each pursued this quest unconsciously and quite differently: Nelson became the daring conqueror whom he believed his mother would admire; Hitler continued to protect his imagined mother by fighting off the ghost of his oppressive father; while Diana, giving up on her mother's love, appealed to the whole world to love her for her beauty and good works.

Maternal loss in childhood is known to change adult life in many ways, often causing marked cognitive, emotional or behavioural problems. It is believed that such losses can interfere with later identity formation and the establishment of self-esteem, and to cause anxiety and depression over many years, especially where grief after bereavement has never been resolved. Fears of further loss can lead to the avoidance of attachment in adulthood. (We see this in Hitler.) More irrationally, but just as commonly, there is anger with the departed mother (as in Diana's case) and guilt—a hidden feeling of responsibility for the mother's disappearance—that we can detect in all our subjects.

Purely by coincidence the three cases of maternal loss described in this book all occurred at Christmas. This is a special time for children from Christian backgrounds. In all three cases, probably, our victims had previously experienced Christmas as an especially happy and magical time. Christmases are occasions when families are typically together and can celebrate the love between mother and child. Mothers, at this season, give presents to their children and, in happy families, it is a time at which children can feel most secure and loved. How especially cruel, therefore, that for Horatio, Adolf and Diana it was also at a Christmas that they all lost their mothers. This fortuitous timing could only have added to the bitterness of their loss.

Anniversaries of major traumas are often important in the world of the unconscious. For all of our subjects Christmas remained an unsettling time of year at which all, as adults, tended to take momentous and sometimes unwise decisions. As we have seen, this was especially true of Nelson who had fallen in love at Christmas 1798, started his sexual affair with Emma the following Christmas, and left his wife at Christmas the year after that. In later life Hitler would also make momentous decisions at Christmas times fired, so it seems, by a do-or-die urge to fight for his mother, maintaining the symbolic 'struggle' with his father at all costs: in December 1941, for example, he unnecessarily and madly declared war on America. Later in the month he ordered his troops to defend the Eastern front to the last man and took over the supreme command of the army himself. On 26 December 1941 Adolf dismissed one of his best generals (Guderian) because he had advised a tactical retreat and on New Year's Eve, after a long and furious argument with another general on the same issue, Adolf bizarrely summoned his secretaries to have tea with him in the middle of the night. Ian Kershaw concludes that the winter of 1941–1942 can now be seen as 'not merely a turning-point, but the beginning of the end'. Exactly a year later Hitler showed the same, perhaps even suicidal, stubbornness in refusing to allow General Paulus to retreat from Stalingrad. On 19 December 1942 he rejected all requests for a break-out and the catastrophe of Stalingrad ensued, Hitler still ordering the army to stand fast 'to the last soldier'. In consequence Paulus had to surrender 113,000 men to the

Russians having already lost 100,000 in a battle he could not have won. Again, it was a massive turning-point in the war that could have been avoided or reduced by a timely retreat. Two years later in December 1944, Hitler's Christmas lunacy was again repeated when he showed the same recklessness and lack of realism by ordering an attempted counterattack against the Allies through the Ardennes to the Channel coast. This was contrary to the advice of all his military commanders. Hitler however believed, so it seems, in the messianic power of his will alone. So on 16 December some 200,000 German troops attacked the Americans. It was now an all-or-nothing struggle, Hitler said, for 'the continued existence of Germany' (symbolically his mother). On 24 December, however, the Ardennes fog lifted exposing the German forces to devastating attack from Allied aircraft, and by early January this last German offensive was all over. Some 80,000 German lives had been unnecessarily lost in a short-lived advance of only some fifteen miles.

Was it a coincidence that Hitler would make these desperate and reckless decisions at Christmas-times? I do not think so. It was all about Christmas 1907 when, despite all his efforts, his mother Klara (i.e., Germany) had died. Now at Christmas 1941, Christmas 1942 and Christmas 1944 it was all being unconsciously repeated in Hitler's fanatical attempts to preserve, as he said, 'the existence of the substance of our German people' (i.e., his mother). If this Christmas madness of Hitler had been diagnosed by the Allies during the war years it could, surely, have been of military use.

Hitler's chronic failure to form proper working relationships with his generals was because they did not fit in with his psychodynamics. Principally he saw them as father-figures and so, instinctively, he fought them. Yet, paradoxically, he also needed them as his chief allies in the greater struggle. Psychopathology was here in direct conflict with reality. It was a dilemma that was never to be resolved—and with fatal consequences for Germany.

Attachment and loss

Over the last fifty years, following the pioneering work of John Bowlby and others, much has been written about attachment and loss. Bowlby described the natural need of children for a secure relationship with an adult caregiver and suggested that the characteristics of such attachment tend to be repeated in adult life. Two main reactions occur in infants when they are temporarily separated from caregivers: attachment-anxiety and attachment-avoidance. Insecure adults repeat this pattern; on one hand are those who, while fearing repeated loss, constantly demand more from their intimate adult relationships (as in Diana's case), and on the other are those who avoid all attachment, preferring not to rely upon others at all. (We could put Hitler in this second category.) This latter group has been traditionally associated with later delinquency, although more recent research has suggested that such attachment-avoidance may sometimes produce genuine resilience and prove to be a useful defence in adulthood.

Bowlby postulated five principal emotional stages of childhood grief following loss:

(1) *Numbing* with occasional outbursts of distress and anger (this lasts from hours to a few days);

(2) *Yearning and searching* for the lost one (this may last for months or years);

(3) *Despair* (Grief);

(4) *Detachment* (sometimes leading to increased narcissism);

(5) *Re-Organisation* (Recovery).

He concluded that recovery can be complete provided that the child is reunited with the lost carer *before* detachment occurs. We can see that all three of our subjects seem to have been stuck in the yearning and searching phase, and with Nelson and Hitler we also see increased narcissism.

Whereas Bowlby's work was based chiefly upon separation and loss in infancy (before the age of thirty months), the three cases in this book describe maternal loss in children between the ages of six and eighteen years. Each case shows catastrophic sensitivity combined with remarkable defensive ingenuity. Neither Hitler nor Nelson could accept the deaths of their mothers. In their inner and largely unconscious fantasy worlds their mothers still existed but needed to be attracted, protected and fought for. Both men longed for their mothers and devoted their whole lives to regaining them. Indeed, both shook the foundations of their worlds to do this. Our subjects are, by definition, unusual cases and for this reason we have heard of them. For this reason, too, we should not assume that their remarkable reactions to the trauma of maternal loss are commonplace or ordinary. In each case the primary reactions of our subjects were in the realms of the imagination, some of it conscious and some of it not so. Hitler was already a practised fantasist before his mother's death and his fantasised attempts to protect her were so elaborate that they included no less than the waging of a world war. Nelson's strategy was to win back his mother's approval by defeating the French, and in the course of this he discovered in Emma Hamilton the perfect mother replacement. Diana was not a mother's favourite as Hitler and Nelson had been and was different from the other two in still having a mother who was alive. But Diana still desperately needed the tactile love that her mother had given her in early childhood and which she felt had been denied her after her parents' divorce. What was shared by all our subjects was that their maternal losses marked a crossroads in their lives and the beginning of momentous journeys that took them to the heights of celebrity and were concluded only at their own deaths. All three were fixated by their traumas. All three were stuck in their childhoods trying to reverse the unbearable calamities of their maternal loss.

The spoiled child

For Hitler and Nelson their traumas had been intensified because they had been their mothers' favourites; the loss of their mothers was therefore all the more terrible for them. Mother's boys (and father's pets) deserve more study than they receive because (as with Hitler) they include the arrogant and angry narcissists who sometimes change the world. They have to do this in order to live up to their doting parent's very high expectations. I suspect that many of the celebrities in the world today are doing what they are doing for this very reason.

This raises the whole question of 'the spoiled child' — a phrase often mentioned in conversation but rarely by psychologists. The concept is loosely applied to children who appear demanding, undisciplined and egocentric. In this sense all three of our subjects could be so described and yet, as we have seen, their upbringings were markedly different. Only Hitler, after the death of his father, can accurately be called a child who was truly spoiled by a doting mother. Although Diana was unused to discipline and had material presents piled upon her, she was in fact emotionally deprived. Nelson, too, although his mother's favourite, was (as far as we know) never spoiled by her. There are at least five separate possible components to parental 'spoiling' — I shall call them overvaluing, pampering, overprotecting, under-controlling and smothering. The overvaluing by a parent gives the child the feeling that it is 'special' and imposes upon it the obligation to achieve. Pampering (the emphasis upon satisfying the child's every need) increases the child's feeling of specialness but, paradoxically, often makes it feel dissatisfied. Overprotecting the child from real and imagined dangers can make it fearful and insecure. Under-controlling produces a demanding child with a sense of power and an intolerance of frustration. Smothering creates either rebellious anger or dependent submission, or both. We can see that Nelson's parenting certainly gave him the feeling that he was special whereas Hitler, being under-controlled by his mother, also developed a love of power that became accentuated by his internalised struggle with his father. In a world of smaller families and only-children these aspects of 'spoiled' and narcissistic children may need closer study in the future.

Narcissism and politics

Narcissism is making rather a comeback in psychological circles. Even in everyday speech the word, defined as meaning 'self-infatuation' or 'excessive admiration for oneself', seems to be ousting the older 'egotism' (speaking too much about oneself), 'egoism' (selfishness) and 'egocentricity' (interest in oneself only). One could say that these ego-based conditions tend to be the *consequences* of narcissism. I have already suggested that Diana was not a narcissist but that Nelson very obviously was one. Hitler went even further and became a narcissistic personality *disorder*. His narcissism showed itself in several ways: his grandiosity, his fantasies of unlimited success, his belief in his own special qualities and in his sense of entitlement from the German people. Like other Utopian cult-leaders he persuaded others to kill in his name, while killing no-one with his own hands except himself. Some might guess that Adolf's grandiose fantasies were a shield against his largely unconscious feelings of failure, disgust and guilt; lack of self-esteem and grandiosity being able to co-exist in narcissists. Hitler was amiable as long as he had his way, but when thwarted or criticised, quite typically for a narcissist, he would react with anger.

What were the origins of Hitler's exceptionally narcissistic personality? There seems to me to be two principal origins for such narcissistic disorders. The first occurs when an abused child feels that no-one appreciates, admires or loves him, so he begins, in self-defence, to love himself, defending all threats to his self-esteem by providing his own fantasies of success and specialness. The second origin is when someone near to him, usually the mother, holds him in very special esteem such as when, in Adolf's case, he is the only surviving son in an unhappy marriage. The son, as it were, simply accepts the mother's judgement and develops a very high opinion of himself. A doting mother (as Adolf had) who considers that her son is someone extraordinary, with special gifts, who can 'do anything' as she said, naturally tends to convince the boy that this is true. He believes her. Consequently he strives to close the gap between his mediocre performances in real life and the over-valued view of himself as 'a man of destiny' that he has acquired from his mother. This is a common feature of 'mother's boys' in general and of many so-called 'great' men such as Churchill and Stalin.

Nelson, too, shows many narcissistic features but, because he was never so sure of his mother's high opinion of him (and because he was never actually abused by his father) they are less extreme. Furthermore, unlike Hitler who was surrounded by a sycophantic nation, Nelson was constantly confronted by the stark realities of life in the Navy. In consequence his narcissism showed itself in the harmless love of praise, medals and titles and never seriously impaired his career or his relationships. Above all, he never showed the inflexibility of Hitler, nor the tendency to repeat mistakes, that are characteristics of a personality disorder.

Certainly there are lessons here for the current century about narcissism and politics. Prime Minister Tony Blair, a one time would-be pop star, lost his mother rather suddenly as he graduated from Oxford and, years earlier, his 'atheistic' father's political career had been abruptly terminated by a stroke. Blair handled both traumas with the help of religion. He evolved into a formidable and celebrity-conscious politician—charismatic and eloquent, but with a worrying tendency to wage wars for messianic purposes. The Iraq war and its subsequent ill-planned aftermath caused the maiming and deaths of thousands of soldiers and civilians. In Europe, repugnance at these effects blotted from memory many of Blair's positive achievements. After leaving office he converted to Roman Catholicism, narcissistically establishing the Tony Blair Faith Foundation in order, so he announced, 'to awaken the world's conscience'. Narcissists have to be recognised and treated with caution, especially when they become politicians who are in a position to affect our lives or destroy them.

Some subtle issues are raised by these interlocking psychobiographies. Although, as David Owen has pointed out, political leaders often display signs of what he calls 'hubris', so also do other celebrities who are not politicians. They, too, can show arrogance and over-confidence, self-obsession and contempt for the advice of others. They, too, can be impulsive, reckless and restless. This fact raises further questions; are these hubristic behaviours the effects of power or of celebrity? Do they only develop in a special personality or are they possible in all personality types? What exactly are the connections between hubristic behaviour, narcissistic personality and hypomania? I will hazard one or two answers to such questions. First, it is celebrity (being the centre of attention rather than having actual power) that tends to produce hubris. We can see this in the case of the old-fashioned 'prima donna'; she can show hubristic arrogance, self-obsession and contempt for the advice of others, even though she has little real power. Hypomania, too, even when it occurs in the non-celebrity can produce similarly hubristic results, and so can the narcissistic personality—although it is possible to argue that such personalities often develop precisely because the child feels it is a celebrity in the eyes of its parent. So I think hubristic behaviour (we could call it 'big-headedness') tends to result just as much from celebrity as from the holding of power itself. Narcissistic personalities are probably attracted to professions where they may find celebrity—football, television or politics, for example. How then do celebrities resist the pressures of hubris? Those who are neither narcissistic nor hypomanic are almost certainly less vulnerable. So also are those from 'showbiz' or ruling class backgrounds where attitudes resistant to hubris have become established. Also more restrained are those with spouses or parents (or even children) who puncture the bubbles of their hubris—as Clementine Churchill had to do with her husband Winston.

Hitler and Churchill

Incidentally, we can see that there are some remarkable psychological similarities between Adolf Hitler and Winston

Churchill. Sometimes the difference between hero and villain is precariously narrow. Both Hitler and Churchill were outstanding and painstaking orators, both were physically slight, both loved art and were actual artists, both were proud of their medal-winning military service and (when young) both were fascinated by war, both were great patriots and imperialists, indeed both greatly esteemed the British Empire, both adored their mothers and had lost their fathers when young, both loved nature and animals (although Winston preferred cats to subservient dogs while Adolf was vice versa), both were charismatic, both had rages, both were afraid of female sexuality, both believed themselves to be 'men of destiny', both revered history, both were successful leaders, both were narcissistic and bipolar (although Churchill's depressions were more severe than Hitler's), and both blamed a conspiracy for most of the world's problems—the Jews in Hitler's case and the Nazis in Churchill's. What, then, made the difference? Churchill was certainly the more thorough historian and had the better sense of humour but, far more importantly, he was part of a culture that highly valued decency, moderation, fair-play, compromise and peace. He was also an aristocrat whose background had equipped him with knowledge of the dangers of power and fanaticism, whereas Hitler's recent peasant background gave him no such warnings. Churchill's psychopathology contained little hatred and permitted him to have warm and admiring relationships with other men. (His father had never beaten him nor openly fought with him.) Churchill was never the loner that Adolf had been and, unlike Hitler he had never so much cultivated his inner world of (messianic) fantasy, although the messianism was present. During the war Churchill learned from his mistakes whereas Hitler did not. Whereas Churchill learned not to overrule his generals Hitler, showing a rigidity typical of a personality disorder, continued to do so. Churchill (like Blair) may have been unconsciously trying to complete his father's interrupted political career whereas Hitler was determined to destroy his father. Churchill was not surrounded by sycophants as

Hitler was, and had a wife, Clementine, who could if necessary bring him down to earth. Whereas Hitler rejected any form of weakness, Churchill was a compassionate man who would fight to *protect* the weak. Above all, the young Churchill had never lost his adored and ambitious mother who had inspired and directed his career; she did not die until he was well into his forties. These were crucial differences.

Dictators

What then makes a dictator? The answer is, nearly always, a narcissistic personality disorder. We see this with Stalin, Franco, Mussolini and Hitler. We often also see similar family backgrounds—a spoiling and overvaluing mother and an oppressive (and sometimes cruel) father. In this present study Hitler is the archetype. He lived in a world of fantasy based upon his love for his mother and his hatred of a brutish father who had frequently beaten him and opposed his artistic and other ambitions. His father's ghost had become, however, in Adolf's mind, the Jews. To an extent Adolf, like other dictators, was expressing his anger and revenge towards his father over and over again, as if never able to obtain permanent relief. Serial killers, often experiencing anger towards their rejecting mothers, act similarly. For them, killings and acts of destruction are cathartic and serve as temporary painkillers. Whereas in the case of these psychopathic murderers such anger usually blots out all feelings of empathy and affection, this did not quite happen in Adolf's case. But he had to continue fighting. *The cause of the Second World War was simply this: he had to keep fighting his father.*

The conflict with his frightening and violent father was also important in the formation of Adolf's character. It accounts for his anger, his obstinacy, his deep lack of self-confidence and, ultimately, for his acceptance of violence as a way to deal with problems. Some of these traits are reactions against the father, while others imitate him. Probably, as I have suggested, the combination of doting mother and violent father is the typical background for dictators. The mother convinces them that they are men of destiny while the hated father provokes their anger against the world and suggests that retaliatory violence is the answer. In Adolf's case, his fears of impotence just made everything worse. He had to find potency through war instead of through more natural channels. The choice of politics, too, was part of his reaction against the father who had despised his oratory.

Despots, no less than torturers or serial murderers, are still human beings. However obnoxious their actions, biographers should not allow their contempt for them to get in the way of establishing the truth. There has been a dangerous tendency simply to demonise Hitler. As Albert Speer noted in his diary as early as 1947—'people are increasingly representing Hitler merely as a dictator given to raging uncontrollably ... ' No, even Adolf was a human being. Therein, precisely, lies the danger.

Understanding Adolf does not, of course, in any way, condone the monstrously evil effects of his regime. Indeed, I hope that it may act as a warning. Adolf did not see himself as evil. On the contrary, he wanted to do good. He was not a true psychopath. Adolf was in some ways a weak person forcing himself to be strong, an Austrian outsider determined to be German, a lazy daydreamer driving himself to be active, a little boy pretending to be a man. We can see that Adolf's personality was paranoid and obsessional as well as narcissistic. But he was not entirely mad. Part of him longed for the war to be over, so that he could retire back to his spaciously redesigned home-town of Linz. He once told Speer—'Aside from Fräulein Braun I'll take no-one with me ... Fräulein Braun and my dog.' With loyal and subservient dogs, and much younger women, he felt relaxed; he did not have to put on any acts to impress them. By the end he was probably fed up with the perpetual role of superman in which he had cast himself. Secretly, he worried endlessly about his health, consulted astrologers and fed his large collection of rare birds, the occasional deaths of which brought tears to his eyes. In the Berlin bunker he actually cried openly on two occasions, so Traudl Junge recalled, once when Eva had refused to leave the bunker for her own safety, and also on the day that they were married. Eva was utterly loyal to him, just as his mother was, or perhaps, should have been, and she admired him almost as much as he did so himself.

For a few months after the Battle of the Nile Nelson, too, had behaved like a little dictator, facilitating the execution of the Neapolitan rebels. Diana, on the other hand, although sometimes waspish to courtiers and to those who tried to structure her lifestyle, resisted the worst temptations of hubris. For her, the necessary narcissism simply was not there. Hitler, though, remains the paradigm of dictatorship – the history of a father and son bitterly and constantly at loggerheads in a struggle that was never to be resolved because of his father's death when Adolf was only thirteen. For his mother's sake he had 'struggled' to defeat the symbol of his father (international Jewry) and failed. Unconsciously in Adolf's mind the Second World War had been this very struggle.

Fantasy

All of us have fantasies – principally the hopes and fears for our future that appear, often disguised, in our dreams. But they are with us always, usually just below the surface of consciousness, influencing our behaviour. There are conscious fantasies too and some people, like Adolf Hitler, live in their active and conscious imagination where fantasies abound, providing for them a refuge from the unpleasantness of the real world. The teenage Adolf seems to have become a bit of a loner, escaping into a world of grandiose and Wagnerian fantasy; which is where, more or less, he stayed for the remainder of his life, still playing out his childhood 'struggle' with his father. Adolf once said that Wagnerian opera was his religion. From his teens onwards he had steeped himself in the music and, more importantly for him, the mythology of the Wagnerian narrative. The sheer spectacle of the operas, their scale and the general ethos of grandeur and heroism that they exuded, also appealed to him. The skinny little school dropout found in Wagner all the magnificence that he lacked. In general, Wagner's overall theme is that of the Germanic hero overcoming the forces of evil. Adolf certainly identified himself with this. To the embarrassment of some Nazi idealogues, Adolf especially loved *Parsifal* with its soft environmental themes, mystical sense of union with nature and its apparent disapproval of sexuality. More publicly, Adolf's favourite was *Rienzi* where the hero rescues a female relative from abduction. The parallel with Adolf's core personal fantasy is obvious. Moreover, both heroes, Parsifal and Rienzi, are eventually killed by their enemies, the latter dying and being consumed by flames, just as Siegfried and Brünnhilde are also in *Götterdämmerung (The Twilight of the Gods)*. The kingdom of the gods is destroyed around them just as the Third Reich was. Did Adolf, ordering his own cremation in Berlin's ruins, see himself in this way? Almost certainly. Is this the reason why he opted to die in Berlin rather than retreat to the South of Germany and give himself up, tamely, to the Americans? Very probably.

Nelson's fantasies of derring-do were conscious but the irrational underlying fantasies of winning back the love of his mother remained beneath the surface. In Diana's case, her principal restitutive fantasy was that marriage to someone very special would be the answer to all her problems. This was, so it seems, very much the effect of her childhood reading of the romantic novels of Barbara Cartland in which the perfect marriage is often depicted as a panacea. In her case these fantasies were quite conscious. What was often unconscious was her continuing yearning for the apparently lost love of her mother and for the cuddling she used to receive in her infancy. This is why, when her marriage did not turn out to be the answer to all her woes, Diana became distraught.

Conclusions

In history, psychology certainly matters. What is more, it matters today in world politics. The West, for example, is obsessed with its so-called 'war on terrorism' but rarely pauses to try to understand the true motives of the terrorists. Their misinterpretations of the religion of Islam are only part of the picture. Far more importantly terrorists are driven by personal anger and revenge, the origins of which will range in each instance from family dynamics (as in Hitler's case) to individual feelings of alienation and failure within their adopted countries in the West, to the senses of frustration and injustice caused by the bad governance of so many (but not all) Islamic states and, above all, to realistic resentment of Western foreign policy especially as regards Palestine. Some terrorists will also be driven by desperate and even suicidal quests for celebrity. Understanding today's history-makers more deeply than we do might help to change the world for the better. Politicians and commentators habitually emphasise the impact of rational political and economic determinants and ignore, to their own disadvantage, the psychological.

We have seen that all three of our subjects were traumatised by the loss of their mothers in childhood. Many lives of extraordinary achievement may have been created in this way—Charles Darwin, for example, also lost his mother in childhood and converted her remembered love of nature into his own earth-shaking career. For our three subjects their lives were, to a great extent, symbolic attempts to recover their lost maternal love. Nelson did this by joining the Navy and by fighting the French. Hitler did so by trying to destroy the Jews (a symbol of his hated father) and by striving to find *lebensraum* for Germany (his mother). Diana's solution was to win the love of the world by showing it how good and beautiful she was. All three wanted the world to admire them. Eventually Nelson succeeded in his emotional quest, not only by defeating the French and receiving the love of his nation, but also by finding the ideal mother-substitute in Emma Hamilton. The other two failed in their missions: Hitler losing his symbolic struggle with his father (i.e., the Second World War) and Diana finding that even the love of the whole world was not enough to conquer her misery.

Sources

Bowlby, John, *Attachment and Loss* (London: Hogarth, 1980)

Kershaw, Ian, *Hitler: 1889–1936: Hubris* (Harmondsworth: Penguin Books, 1998)

Kershaw, Ian, *Hitler: 1936–1945: Nemesis* (Harmondsworth: Penguin Books, 2000)

Junge, Traudl, *Until the Final Hour – Hitler's Last Secretary* ed. Melissa Müller, (Munich: Ullstein Heyne, 2002), English tr. Anthea Bell (London: Weidenfeld & Nicolson, 2003)

Milgram, Stanley, *Obedience to Authority: An Experimental View* (London: Harper Collins 1974)

Owen, David, *In Sickness and in Power: Illness in Heads of Government During the Last 100 Years* (London: Methuen, 2008)

Schultz, William Todd ed., *Handbook of Psychobiography* (Oxford: Oxford University Press, 2005)

Glossary

Bipolar disorder Episodes of mania (or hypomania) alternating with episodes of depression.

Borderline Personality disorder A personality disorder characterized by a severely impaired capacity for attachment often with paranoid ideas, intense anger, suicidal gestures, impulsivity, anxiety, unstable judgements of others, uncertain self-image and fears of abandonment.

Bulimia Repeated bouts of overeating and an excessive preoccupation with body-weight.

Depression Abnormally low or depressed mood with loss of enjoyment, impaired concentration, low self-esteem, reduced energy, ideas of guilt or hopelessness, suicidal thoughts and sleep disturbance.

Hubris Syndrome Proposed by David Owen in 2006 to describe the excessive self-confidence, restlessness, recklessness, impulsiveness, inattention to detail, contempt for the advice of others and messianic thinking sometimes to be found in political leaders.

Hypomania A lesser degree of mania.

Mania Abnormally elevated mood, either euphoric or irritable, showing increased energy, reduced sleep, grandiosity, loss of normal inhibitions, pressure of speech, flight of ideas and impaired concentration.

Narcissistic Personality disorder A personality disorder characterized by a need for excessive admiration, grandiosity, arrogance, envy, lack of empathy, a sense of 'entitlement', feelings of specialness, fantasies of brilliance and achievement, and a tendency to exploit others.

Oedipus Complex Sigmund Freud's term for excessive attachment to the opposite sex parent and rivalry with the same-sex parent. In Freud's opinion such childhood experiences are the origin of most neurosis.

Personality disorder Deeply ingrained and enduring behaviour patterns that tend to be inflexible and out of the ordinary for the given culture, often causing distress for the sufferer or for others.

Transference Tendency to transfer feelings and expectations experienced in important childhood relationships onto others in later life, often quite inappropriately.